Robert,

Continue to follow the
Wisdom of our Ancestors!

2012

Praise for *Grandma's Hands*

"This book is a treasure, one that everyone will enjoy sharing. The images portray the beauty of love across generations. The passages honor the wisdom and solid values that are indeed timeless. Together, *Grandma's Hands* is a visual and spiritual feast! I love it."

Dr. Carolyn W. Meyers, Ph.D.

President
Jackson State University
Jackson, MS

"With eyes of faith, Dr. Mackie peers into the 'soul' of the wise grandmother and cleverly extracts the most salient and timeless truths, which both affirm and challenge the content of one's character. In doing so, he perpetually inspires generations to succeed against the odds with enduring images of hope. These hope-filled reflections eloquently penned in *Grandma's Hands* are invaluable, and they are a refreshing rediscovery of sayings of grandmothers throughout the ages."

The Rev. Kendrick E. Curry, Ph.D., MDiv

Senior Pastor
The Pennsylvania Avenue Baptist Church
Washington, DC

"Dr. Mackie's book provides a bit of solace and sanctity sorely needed for the times in which we live. It captures the very essence of the wisdom, guidance, and instruction of generations past. Job well done!"

Elder Lynette M. Doyle

Founder/Executive Director
NtheGap Ministries

"We are unfortunately living in an era of an "un-raised" generation where wise words are virtually unspoken and thus unknown. The words of wisdom that reared generation upon generation are seemingly null and void. Thankfully, Dr. Calvin Mackie has masterfully recovered many of the age-old wisdom sayings—yes, the life lessons that have encouraged, directed, corrected, challenged, and sustained so many generations. Coupled with the Word of God, these "Grandma's proverbs" connect us with biblical prophetic certainty while providing a blessed assurance for our present reality and an unwavering hope for our future. *Grandma's Hands* enables us to reflect, to relive, to renew, and most of all to remember what Grandmamma said—sayings that never become outdated or obsolete but stay with us and continue to instruct us for a lifetime."

Father Maurice J. Nutt, C.Ss.R., D.Min.

Catholic Evangelist, Homiletics Professor,
Author, and Motivational Speaker
Chicago, IL

"This book captures the central role that grandmothers play in our lives. Regardless of race, religion or ethnic background, grandmothers hold a special place in our hearts, and memories. Those reassuring words, countless prayers, and soft hands have shaped me into the man I have become. Even today when I am faced with a difficult decision, I still ask myself, "Would my grandmother be proud of the choice I have made?" Words could not express, nor could numbers quantify the impact that my grandmother has had on my life. *Grandma's Hands* is the closest I have ever come to capturing what my grandma means to me. I applaud Dr. Mackie for putting pen to paper to describe what grandmothers mean to most of us."

Sam Johnson

Managing Partner
Ernst & Young LLP

Grandma's Hands

Cherished Moments of Faith and Wisdom

Calvin Mackie, Ph.D.

Published by Acanthus Publishing, Boston, Massachusetts.

Photo credits:

© istockphoto.com:

Aldo Murillo: 24, 40, 41, 222, 223, 224, 225
ALEAIMAGE: 114
Amanda Rohde: 87
Andres Peiro Palmer: 72
Ann Marie Kurtz: 202, 221, 222
anne de Haas: 31
Arash James Iravan: 94
Barbara Reddoch: 196
Bartosz Hadyniak: 85, 169
beccazpa: 11
Benoit Beauregard: 143
best-photo: 30, 31
Bob Thomas: 39
bonnie jacobs: 74
Brian Toro: 119

Carme Balcells: 36
Christopher Futcher: 22, 23
CJMGrafx: 29
Cliff Parnell: 90, 122, 131, 172, 173, 177, 204, 206
Dan Moore: 191
Daniel Laflor: 44, 64
David Sucsy: 128
dblight: cover, 10, 51
Debstreasures: 26
Derek Latta: 56, 82
Diana Lundin; 81
Diane Diederich: 95
digitalskillet: 10, 89, 93, 162, 163, 193, 218
Don Bayley: 195
Eduardo Jose Bernardino: 29, 192

Evelyn Peyton: 184
Eward Bock: 172
Flashon Studio: 214
gokhan ilgaz: 19
hanhanpeggy: 50
iofoto: 103
Izabela Habur: 112
Jacob Wackerhausen: 116, 117, 160, 205
James Richey: 170
Jeanine Groenewald: 43
Jeffrey Banke: 35
Josef Vital: 68, 151
jozef sedmak: 42
Juanmonino: 49
Kai Chiang: 86
kali9: 60, 98, 99, 154, 155

Kathy Dewar: 108
Kathye Killer: 46
Ke Yu: 133
Kemter: 135
Kevin Russ: 72, 220
Konstantin Sutyagin: 153, 159
kristian sekulic: 70, 71
laurent Renault: 28
Lisa F. Young: 108, 134, 166, 212, 213
Marcela Barsse: 148
Martina Ebel: 114
Michelle Gibson: 25, 144
Miguel Malo: 183
Miodrag Gajic: 57
Monique Harris: 150
monkeybusinessimages: 67, 104,

105, 124, 125, 198, 199
Nancy Louie: 126
narvikk: 150
ND1939: 146, 147
Nikolay Mamluke: 96
Neustockimages: 178
orangelinemedia: 53
Özgür Donmaz: 27, 174
Plus: 68
poco_bw: 140
quavondo: 188
Rich Legg: 152, 153
RonTech2000: 209, 219
Rudyanto Wijaya: 63
ShaneKato: 34
Slobodan Vasic: 216
Stuart Monk: 10

Sunitha Pilli: 54
Suprijono Suharjoto: 77
Tatiana Gladskikh: 37
Terry J Alcorn: 136, 137
THEGIFT777: 78, 167
VanDenEsker: 214, 215
VikramRaghuvanshi: 16, 32, 90, 91, 94, 100, 156, 186, 187, 210
Warwick Lister-Kaye: 102
wavebreakmedia: 20
Willie B. Thomas: 46, 47, 120
YinYang: 201, 224

Table of Contents

Dedication

This book is dedicated to my mother, Martha Gordon Mackie, and Tracy's mother, Birtena McQuarter Ransom:

Martha Gordon Mackie (May 14, 1942 – May 30, 1994)

Your wisdom and uncompromising faith in God continue to serve as the headlights in the fog of life's constant challenges. It is our hope that your lives, as virtuous women, loving mothers, and respected grandmothers serve as an example for all who pick up this book. It was you who trained your children in the way we should go and we shall never depart from it. Through this book, we share your everlasting wisdom and guidance with the world. We watched as you did at least one good deed every day and your food fed not only your family, but the community and the homeless too. To you, we say thank you. You embody what the Bible called a virtuous woman in Proverbs 31:10-31:

Who can find a virtuous woman? for her price is far above rubies.

The heart of her husband doth safely trust in her, so that he shall have no need of spoil.

She will do him good and not evil all the days of her life.

She seeketh wool, and flax, and worketh willingly with her hands.

She is like the merchants' ships; she bringeth her food from afar.

She riseth also while it is yet night, and giveth meat to her household, and a portion to her maidens.

She considereth a field, and buyeth it: with the fruit of her hands she planteth a vineyard.

She girdeth her loins with strength, and strengtheneth her arms.

She perceiveth that her merchandise is good: her candle goeth not out by night.

She layeth her hands to the spindle, and her hands hold the distaff.

She stretcheth out her hand to the poor; yea, she reacheth forth her hands to the needy.

She is not afraid of the snow for her household: for all her household are clothed with scarlet.

She maketh herself coverings of tapestry; her clothing is silk and purple.

Her husband is known in the gates, when he sitteth among the elders of the land.

She maketh fine linen, and selleth it; and delivereth girdles unto the merchant.

Strength and honour are her clothing; and she shall rejoice in time to come.

She openeth her mouth with wisdom; and in her tongue is the law of kindness.

She looketh well to the ways of her household, and eateth not the bread of idleness.

Her children arise up, and call her blessed; her husband also, and he praiseth her.

Many daughters have done virtuously, but thou excellest them all.

Birtena McQuarter Ransom (Feb 11, 1934 – Aug 24, 1995)

Favour is deceitful, and beauty is vain: but a woman that feareth the LORD, she shall be praised.

Give her of the fruit of her hands; and let her own works praise her in the gates.

Calvin & Tracy Mackie

Grandma's Hands

Lyrics by Bill Withers

Grandma's hands
Clapped in church on Sunday morning
Grandma's hands
Played a tambourine so well
Grandma's hands
Used to issue out a warning
She'd say, "Billy, don't you run so fast"
"Might fall on a piece of glass"
"Might be snakes there in that grass"
Grandma's hands

Grandma's hands
Soothed a local unwed mother
Grandma's hands
Used to ache sometimes and swell
Grandma's hands
Used to lift her face and tell her,
"Baby, Grandma understands
That you really love that man
Put yourself in Jesus' hands"
Grandma's hands

Grandma's hands
Used to hand me piece of candy
Grandma's hands
Picked me up each time I fell
Grandma's hands
Boy, they really came in handy
She'd say, "Matty don' you whip that boy
What you want to spank him for?
He didn' drop no apple core"
But I don't have Grandma anymore

If I get to Heaven I'll look for
Grandma's hands

Foreword

By Grandma's House

There are some things in life that you never forget. No matter your age. No matter your race. No matter your education. No matter your denomination. No matter your gender. No matter your vocation. No matter what side of the track you grew up on. There are just some things in life you never forget.

One of those things in my life is the time I spent by my grandmother's house! I am now in my mid 50s; however, I remember like yesterday the great times I spent by my grandmother's house. As my mind goes into rewind mode, there are so many memories of being by "Moma" that I can probably write a book (however, I will leave that to Dr. Mackie)!

My grandmother lived one block from my elementary and junior high schools. So every day, while walking the five blocks to and from school, I stopped by my grandmother's house on the way there and then on the way home. Each day I was given a treat— from homemade biscuits in the morning to baked sweet potatoes in the afternoons. Man, I miss those days! However, the best time spent by grandma's house was during the summer months when all the grandkids would go by grandma's on Friday nights. That was

the night that all the grandkids took time turning the crank on the tub as we made homemade ice cream, and then heard grandmother tell stories about all of our parents from when they were kids! We laughed so hard until we were crying! Those were cherished moments I will never forget and never wanted to end.

In his newest book, *Grandma's Hands: Cherished Moments of Faith and Wisdom*, Dr. Calvin Mackie brings all of us back to those days by grandma's house. As you read this book, be prepared to laugh, to cry, but most of all to remember how much you miss your grandma. I cannot speak for you, but I sure miss mine!

Fred Luter Jr.

Pastor, Franklin Avenue Baptist Church
New Orleans, LA

Vice President, Southern Baptist Convention

Listen, friends, to some fatherly advice; sit up and take notice so you'll know how to live.

Proverbs 4:1

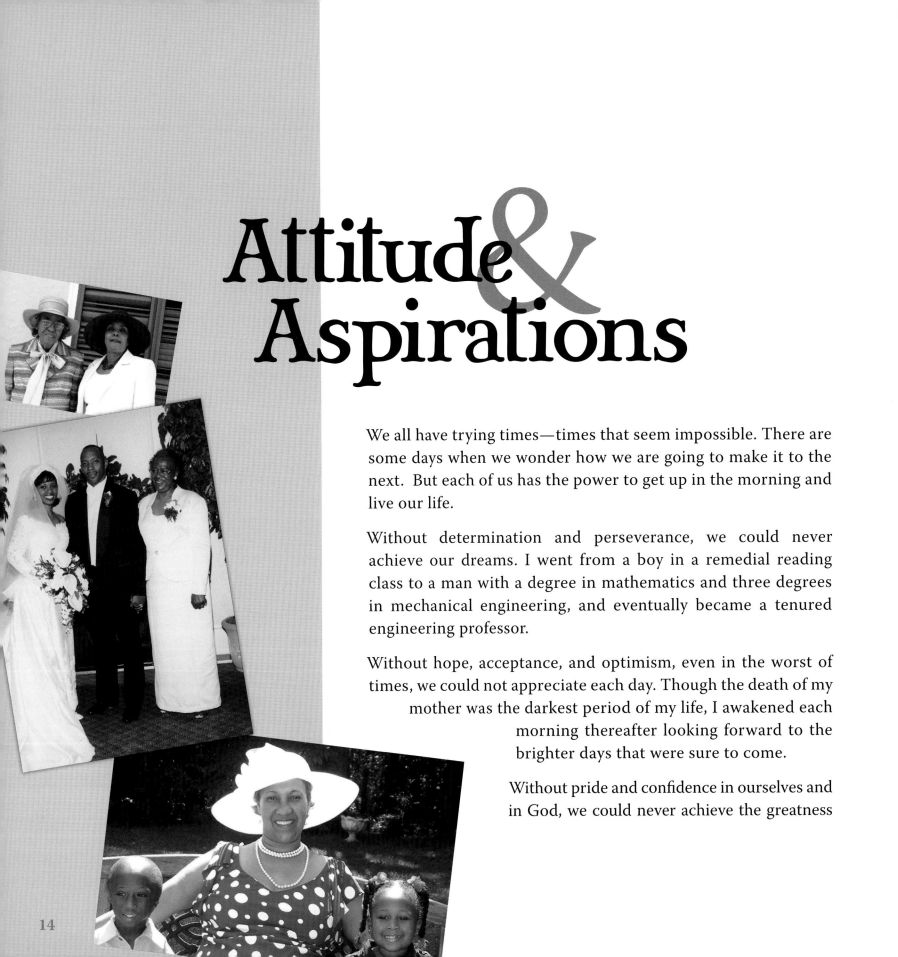

Attitude & Aspirations

We all have trying times—times that seem impossible. There are some days when we wonder how we are going to make it to the next. But each of us has the power to get up in the morning and live our life.

Without determination and perseverance, we could never achieve our dreams. I went from a boy in a remedial reading class to a man with a degree in mathematics and three degrees in mechanical engineering, and eventually became a tenured engineering professor.

Without hope, acceptance, and optimism, even in the worst of times, we could not appreciate each day. Though the death of my mother was the darkest period of my life, I awakened each morning thereafter looking forward to the brighter days that were sure to come.

Without pride and confidence in ourselves and in God, we could never achieve the greatness

How Do You View Life?
What Will Make You Successful?

within. I know that God has set me on this path in life because I am now capable of achieving more things than I ever imagined on my own accord.

All of us must have faith. We simply must rise to whatever challenge faces us with the knowledge that we have been impregnated with greatness and all that we need is within us. As the poet Maltbie D. Babcock says:

"Be strong!

We are not here to play, to dream, to drift;

We have hard work to do and loads to lift;

Shun not the struggle—face it;

'tis God's gift."

When the occasion arises, the proverb arises.

West Africa

This too Shall Pass

Everyone has storms that come into their lives. No one is immune to bad days, or months, or sometimes even years. The best thing we can remember about trouble is that the trouble didn't come to stay.

There were times when life was hard for me—financially, physically, and psychologically—but I took solace in the fact that these bad times were only temporary. I knew that if I could hold on and keep moving forward, better times would come. Bad times had come before, and they had passed, so the present challenges were soon to pass also.

If I didn't understand this proverb before, the events of Hurricane Katrina made it crystal clear. The people of New Orleans took one gut punch after another. First there was the hurricane, then the flood, the government's slow response, the loss of homes, lives, investments, and way of life; and yet, the people knew that all this would pass and life must go on. So years later, when everyone has moved on and the cameras have departed, the people of New Orleans are still rebuilding their lives and city, and eventually the impact of Katrina will pass.

We have a lot to learn from these brave people. I learned it first from Grandma.

Then they cried unto the LORD in their trouble, and he saved them out of their distresses.

Psalm 107:13

> Now we see but a poor reflection as in a mirror; then we shall see face to face. Now I know in part; then I shall know fully, even as I am fully known.
>
> 1 Corinthians 13:12

You Will Understand it Better By & By

We often do not understand why something happened, especially when it has happened to us. I believe everything happens for a reason and there is a lesson to be learned from every event in our lives. However, sometimes the lesson will be revealed over time after we have had more life experiences.

There are tremendous things about my father that I now understand since I have been able to face the world as an adult. Sometimes I thought he did not love me based on his actions; now, later in life, I understand it was pure love that compelled him to do what he did. It was not his responsibility to be my friend, but rather to be my father, a provider, and a protector.

All that Glitters is not Gold

In today's society, undue emphasis is placed on the way someone looks. We are obsessed with the cars we drive, the clothes we wear, and the jewelry adorning us, without ever considering the character of the individual beneath. A person's or item's appearance does not say anything about their essence. Looking through magazines I would always "ooh" and "aah" over the beautiful, scantily-clad women oozing from the pages—and my mother would just continue what she was doing, reiterating, "Everything that glitters is not gold." Many people have bought duds from used car lots because the car looked good, but they never thought to examine the engine. Always look beneath the surface; there's always more there.

> But the LORD said to Samuel, "Do not look at his appearance or at the height of his stature, because I have rejected him; for GOD sees not as man sees, for man looks at the outward appearance, but the LORD looks at the heart."
>
> 1 Samuel 16:7

Strength and honour are her clothing; and she shall rejoice in time to come. She openeth her mouth with wisdom; and in her tongue is the law of kindness.

Proverbs 31:25-26

There's More Than One Way to Skin a Cat

What happens when you chart out your life goals, complete with timelines and specific destinations... and you don't meet them? If you're that focused, you probably get easily stressed. Instead, understand this: there are always numerous ways to accomplish a task at hand. People often argue about how something should be done without realizing that multiple ways are correct.

As a mathematician and engineer, I have had to examine various correct methods for solving the same problem. Never think that you are trapped because your first attempt failed. If one way fails, there is always another way to accomplish your goal. Some people have destroyed their lives believing that they could only be successful if they could attend the best school in the area; when the rejection letter arrived, they gave up on the goal of being successful. Instead, why not find another institution that can take you to that same goal? There are always multiple routes to get to the same destination—but you'll have to do some digging, some examination, to find those alternate paths.

Sticks and Stones May Break Your Bones But Words Will Never Hurt You

Reckless words pierce like a sword, but the tongue of the wise brings healing.

Proverbs 12:18

This proverb cuts in two different ways. Cutting, harsh words from anyone—friend, family, or foe—should never deter or discourage you. You can't really help how your body responds to a physical assault—certain natural laws come into play, and the breaking of skin and bone is sometimes an unavoidable reality—but you can control how your mind responds to assaults of words and attitudes.

But there is a cautionary tale inherent in this proverb: be careful how you talk to other people. No matter how much you tell people that they should not be hurt by others' words, people are hurt by others' words. Make sure that your words are not the ones that cause discouragement, anger, or heartbreak. Remember that words are powerful.

It's Not How You **Start** But How You **Finish**

We live in a world where people judge each other at every turn. Many times we look around at our present condition and make judgments on what we can accomplish. My father accomplished great things in his life with a limited eighth-grade education from state-approved segregated Negro schools—a feat which I will always be proud of, as will his other descendents. However, he frequently belabored the fact that he did not have the education that I was able to achieve. If he had instead focused on what he accomplished, given his challenging origins, he would have seen the victory that all of us see. Booker T. Washington said, "Success is not so much measured by the position one has reached in life, but by the obstacles which he has overcome." We all can accomplish great things regardless of how humble our beginnings are. We cannot begin to dictate where we end up. The journey we have to travel to get to our goal is the most important part—not the actual destination.

Don't Cry Over Spilled Milk

That's Water Under the Bridge

When we make a mistake or someone wrongs us, we have to take the attitude that once it has passed, it is *past*. Why try to do anything about it if it's over and done with and can't be altered? Accept that the water is under the bridge and move on.

Now I'm not talking about things that you can go back and correct. By all means you should challenge wrongs committed against you and correct wrongs you have done. But many times we spend undue energy worrying about or considering things that simply happened, even when they have no feasible remedy. Let this reality go, plan around it if you must, but keep moving toward your dreams and goals. What has already happened is yesterday's news; throw it away like yesterday's paper!

*Forget about what's happened;
don't keep going over old history.*

— Isaiah 43:18 MSG

29

We'll Cross that Bridge
When We Get to It

The sluggard says, "There is a lion outside; I will be killed in the streets!"

Proverbs 22:13 NAS

Many a plan has died in its initial stages due to excessive time spent worrying about things that have not yet presented themselves. Get up every day and work hard toward whatever it is you are attempting to accomplish.

People say that they will not apply for a certain job because they may not get it. This proverb says instead, "Apply and deal with the rejection if it comes." Make your plan, work the plan, and deal with issues as they appear; you cannot plan for everything all the time.

Therefore do not worry about tomorrow, for tomorrow will worry about itself. Each day has enough trouble of its own.

Matthew 6:34 NIV

31

The Grass Always Looks Greener on the Other Side

Our neighbors or friends are always doing better than us—or so it seems. We have weeds in our lawn, but our neighbor's lawn seems perfect—until we look past the façade. Every individual, every situation, every business has its "issues."

Some people jump around from partner to partner and job to job looking for that non-existent utopia, but you have to make the best of your situation and not worry about what is happening next door. If you do move on, make the decision based on what you feel you can or cannot do. If we make all of our decisions based upon our neighbors, it will be like chasing the wind—we will never achieve our dream.

Then I observed that most people are motivated to success by their envy of their neighbors.

Ecclesiastes 4:4

33

It is Always Darkest Before Dawn

It Always Gets Worse Before it Gets Better

Professionally and personally, many of us have had dark days, the kind of days we never want to relive or experience again. I will never forget April 3, 1994, the day my mother called me and told me she had been diagnosed with terminal breast cancer; nor will I forget May 31, 1994, the day she passed away. These were very dark days in my life. Every day I would awaken and know that I had to keep going and that brighter days were coming. Well, the good thing is that those dark days didn't come to stay. Although it usually gets worse before it gets better, we can always know that a brighter day and time are coming. It is when we are convinced that it cannot get any worse that we lean on this proverb to tell us that dawn will bring a different day and a better time.

Weeping may endure for a night, but joy cometh in the morning.

Psalm 30:5

From there Elisha went up to Bethel. As he was walking along the road, some youths came out of the town and jeered at him. "Go on up, you baldhead!" they said. "Go on up, you baldhead!" He turned around, looked at them, and called down a curse on them in the name of the LORD. Then two bears came out of the woods and mauled forty-two of the youths.

2 Kings 2:23-24

God Don't Like Ugly!

No, it's not that God doesn't like "ugly" people. Remember, we've already established that God looks at the heart, not the physical appearance. It's that an "ugly" attitude is rarely rewarded. "Ugly" in this proverb means acting "evil"—constant complaining, undercutting other people, cheating—or doing those things that you know in your gut are not becoming. Grandma is telling us that we will not "get away" with ugliness. The laws of the universe say that ugly behavior will not go unpunished. Above is a sober example from the Bible. If Grandma read this passage of Scripture to you, she'd simply say, "See?"

If Only He Can
Make It
Through the Night

Grandmothers know things that we don't know. One of those things is that there is always something special about the morning and a new day. My grandma would always say that about someone who was very ill in the hospital: "If only he or she can make it through the night." Invariably, she would be right, and often someone who thrashed and moaned during the night would be miraculously better in the morning. When you're having a time of "night," take heart: if you can just "make it through," there will be another side, a "daytime" for you. In the Scriptures, day is nearly always associated with joy, beginnings, newness, and hope. After all, if the day doesn't come, what is the alternative?

It is of the LORD's mercies that we are not consumed, because his compassions fail not. His mercies are new every morning: great is thy faithfulness.

Lamentations 3:22-23

The Blacker the Berry the Sweeter the Juice

In the 1960s, when the phrase "Black is Beautiful" came into popularity with the Black Power Movement, there were those who felt this term reflected a certain "anti-white" sentiment. Nothing could have been further from the truth.

We shouldn't forget that African Americans were castigated and lampooned in minstrel shows that featured white comedians in blackface with exaggerated features, acting impish and ignorant. Our hair was never straight enough, our lips were too big, our women's hips were too wide… The list of criticisms was endless.

And so this phrase, "Black is Beautiful," is a reaction to the intense hatred spewed upon people of African descent, a hatred that even pitted people of color against one another. It represents a celebration of the deeper-hued individuals in God's creation, a recognition that everything God made is sacred and should be honored as such. When Grandma said that, everyone walked a little taller!

…I am fearfully and wonderfully made…

Psalm 139:14

If God is for Me, Who Can Be Against Me?

Recently, I went to an urban high school to give a speech. I was accompanied by four associates from my sponsoring company. As the students filed into the auditorium, out of order, chaotic and disrespectful, cursing and shouting, one of my associates leaned over to me and confided that she was scared. I told her I had faith because I was ordained by God to be there at that moment to speak to those kids. I told her that faith and fear both attract: fear attracts the negative and faith attracts the positive. I stood and spoke on faith, knowing God was with me, and the students responded with respect and positivity. God was for me and those students, so I had nothing to fear—I knew they were not against me.

My grandma always told me that God plus one equals a majority. You are made by God, specially designed by God to fill His unique and special purpose for your life. He is always for you, as long as you are walking in His purposes. And who is God? He is all-powerful. He can do anything. He can be your shield, your protection, the One who tells you when to get up, when to turn around, when to go right, when to go left. He can lead you to the real gold of your life, that thing that will get you excited every morning, ready to face the day regardless of your circumstances. So who's against you? What's his or her name again? If God is for you, you won't even remember!

If GOD be for us, who can be against us?

Romans 8:31

43

The Race is Not Won by the Swiftest or the Strongest

But by he or she who Endures it to the End

This saying goes hand-in-hand with the term "flash in the pan," and with the story of the tortoise and the hare. You know these types of people: they seem powerful; they brag, they boast, they throw their weight around, and they're loud. That was the hare. He seemed as if he had it all over the tortoise; he was certainly faster, and he let the tortoise know it. He was so confident, however, that he let his guard down and decided to take a little rest. After all, the slow tortoise would never catch up. Or would he?

Do you remember the ending? The tortoise made it over the finish line just ahead of the hare. He wasn't intimidated by the hare's bragging or by his speed. He just worked his program his way. Most importantly, he stayed the course. He didn't give up because the hare was so much faster. He just kept going, consistently, without stopping, until he reached the finish line.

You will find that the big "flashers" rarely end up ahead. The individual who is consistent, steady, and dependable is the one who ultimately gets the attention. Don't worry about the so-called "star"—just continue your plan (make sure you have a plan!). Remember: endurance is just another word for faith.

...he that endureth to the end shall be saved.

Matthew 10:22

45

Don't Let the
Right Hand
Know What
the Left One is
Doing

Don't always show your hand, especially with those who are in control of your future, be they teachers, bosses, or coworkers. On the job, don't tell your boss, supervisor, or coworker everything that you are doing or planning to do, because they may use it against you. If you're planning to leave the company, quit the client, or go for that promotion, don't broadcast it. Do your job with one hand and plan your future (or exit) with the other hand.

But when you give to the needy, do not let your left hand know what your right hand is doing.

Matthew 6:3

Mama May Have and Daddy May Have But God Bless the Child Who Has His Own

> "The person who sins will die. The son will not bear the punishment for the father's iniquity, nor will the father bear the punishment for the son's iniquity; the righteousness of the righteous will be upon himself, and the wickedness of the wicked will be upon himself."
>
> Ezekiel 18:20

There were times when I wanted my parents to pay for something for me—when they refused, I would mumble under my breath: "Then I'll do it myself," falling right into the direction of independence and responsibility that they intended for me. However, my utterance would send my mother into a conniption as she recited this proverb. As a kid, I saved every penny that came my way and was rarely without money. This frugality gave me a certain amount of liberty, a liberty that I still enjoy even today. It is the mothers' and fathers' responsibility to provide for their children, but when a child matures to a place where she can support herself or, even better, help her parents, then that is truly God's blessing.

But it's not just money that the child who matures into an adult needs to have. It's her own life. As Grandma would say, you can't go to heaven on your mother's faith. You must have your own.

Lazy hands make a man poor but diligent hands bring wealth.

—— Proverbs 10:4

The Early Bird Gets the Worm

Nothing comes to a sleeper but a dream.

The nationally-known Dr. Howard Adams wrote a book entitled *Get Up with Something on Your Mind!*. It's a collection of life's lessons taught to him by his ancestors. I find the title very appealing and revealing because I was taught that, as a man, every day I had to get up and go get it.

My father was truly an entrepreneur and believed in the "cave man" theory of success: every day you have to get up and go kill or you do not eat. He taught me not to lie in bed in the morning because there was a world to conquer. The person who gets out often and early will win the battle and kill the most food. Nothing comes to a sleeper but a dream. Dr. Martin Luther King Jr. was not assassinated because he had a dream; he was assassinated because every day he awakened and tried to turn his dreams into reality. Wake up early with your future, dreams, family, and life on your mind and go forward about the business of achieving your goals and turning them into reality.

...it is light that makes everything visible. This is why it is said: Wake up, O sleeper, rise from the dead...

Ephesians 5:14

48

Don't
Pick Your Fruit
From the Ground.
Reach Up

Do not ever just settle for what is available. As creations of God, all of us deserve the best in our lives and we should go for it. Do not settle for other people's leftovers; go for style and class.

When you select a mate or partner, step up, reach up, and select someone who can make you better. Do not go backwards and find yourself rearing someone who may not ever mature. Many women believe that they can "fix" men or force them to grow up, and we all know the ending to that story. Like fruit, pick your mate from the batch that has matured at the proper time.

There's a joke that an old lady told me one day that I have never forgotten: she asked, "What is the difference between men and government bonds?" I responded, "I don't know." She said, "Bonds eventually mature." We see men who refuse to grow up and have fallen from the tree, from their parents' home, and are waiting for someone to pick them up. Do not pick your fruit from the ground, that which has fallen from the tree and has lost all ability to grow and further develop. You deserve better.

You Can Lead a Horse to Water But You Cannot Make him Drink

In the aftermath of Hurricane Katrina, the world was shocked as New Orleanians waited on street corners and rooftops for the government and others to save them. People have put forth many reasons as to why this transpired. However, very few people will even discuss the responsibility of the individuals in this matter for fear of criticism for "blaming the victims." The government was absolutely wrong for taking five days to get to New Orleans, but the people must accept some responsibility for their situation. The Mayor, Governor, and the President were on national television days before the storm imploring people to evacuate to a place of safety. Moreover, living in New Orleans, everyone knew the dire predictions of what might happen if a catastrophic hurricane were to strike. People called family members and begged them to leave, but many refused to listen or respond. We can take them to the water, show them the water, but we can't make them drink. Eight percent of New Orleans' population was brought to the water and refused to drink, and so suffered the consequences—ninety-two percent took heed and safely evacuated the city prior to the storm's landfall. Like my father used to say, "I can explain it to you but I can't understand for you."

One who was there had been an invalid for thirty-eight years. When Jesus saw him lying there and learned that he had been in this condition for a long time, he asked him, "Do you want to get well?" "Sir," the invalid replied, "I have no one to help me into the pool when the water is stirred. While I am trying to get in, someone else goes down ahead of me." Jesus said to him, "Get up! Pick up your mat and walk." At once the man was cured; he picked up his mat and walked.

John 5:5-8

Cast your bread
upon the waters,
for after many
days you will
find it again.
Give portions
to seven, yes to
eight, for you
do not know
what disaster
may come upon
the land.

Ecclesiastes 11:1-2

Don't Put All Your Eggs in One Basket

Investing and the stock market have always intrigued me, and I have been investing since I was 24 years old. I started small, putting $25 a month in Intel, McDonald's, and Home Depot, stocks that I still own to this day. I committed to saving/investing at least $100 a month for a lifetime and check it every ten years to see the progress. Well, these are blue-chip stocks and have held their own even after the turbulent days of the market crash. I also put some money in other stocks which were not as stable and did not fare as well during the downturn. I often think about the fact that I would have lost everything had I invested all the money in one place. I was taught to only bet on the race you are running and never allow one person to create your world, because they will always create it too small. Spread your savings out so that one event cannot bring financial catastrophe to your household.

In 2002, I received tenure as a mechanical engineering professor at Tulane University. Tenure is like a guarantee of employment for life; to lose a tenured position, one would have to do something very damaging to the university or the profession. At my tenure celebration, my father came over and congratulated me. "I hear that this means you have a job for life," he said. Then, he taught. "There is no such thing as a guaranteed job for life," he explained. He counseled me to never depend on anyone else to take care of me (that is, pay me) for the rest of my life. He said, "Son, it doesn't seem right; it doesn't make sense." In essence he was saying "Don't put all your eggs in one basket," or depend on one institution or source of income. He must have known something; in the aftermath of Hurricane Katrina, the president of Tulane University claimed financial exigency, which allowed him to cut programs. He decided to keep the football team and eliminate the engineering program, thus terminating my "guaranteed" job. Had I put all my eggs in one basket or thought I would be at Tulane forever, my family and I would have been challenged and stressed; however, I had listened to my father, heeded this proverb, and sustained multiple incomes. There are really no guarantees.

Never place all your faith, belief, or money in one person or institution.

No One
Can Take Your
Education
Away From You

Put Something in Your Head and No One Can Take That From You

The material things that you acquire—cars, homes, and clothes—will never be more important than those non-material riches that cannot be perceived with the five senses. That's what Grandma meant. She knew that true education imparts wisdom, and that the value of that wisdom was worth all the money in the world. In fact, she understood that this kind of wisdom could actually lead to the material things that we seem so bent on grasping. Your education is something you own, something you work for and earn. No one can go inside of your head and pull that knowledge back out—unless you let them.

After Hurricane Katrina devastated New Orleans and I lost my job, I was able to care for my family because while I had lost many physical things—cars, house, clothes—I still had my education, which allowed me and others to bounce back quickly and take care of family. Your education and skills are yours forever.

> Receive my instruction, and not silver; and knowledge rather than choice gold.
>
> Proverbs 8:10

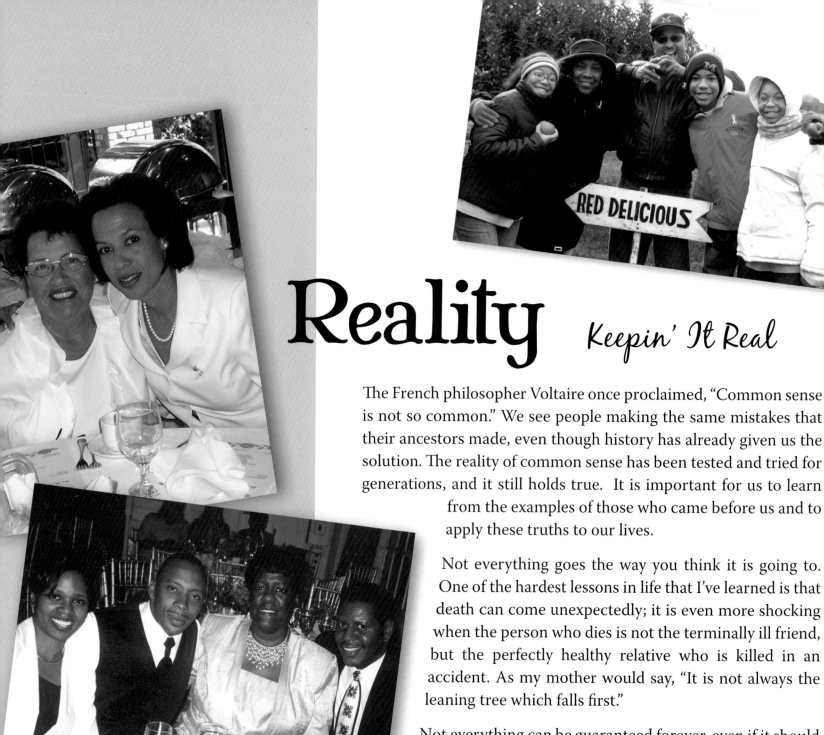

Reality

Keepin' It Real

The French philosopher Voltaire once proclaimed, "Common sense is not so common." We see people making the same mistakes that their ancestors made, even though history has already given us the solution. The reality of common sense has been tested and tried for generations, and it still holds true. It is important for us to learn from the examples of those who came before us and to apply these truths to our lives.

Not everything goes the way you think it is going to. One of the hardest lessons in life that I've learned is that death can come unexpectedly; it is even more shocking when the person who dies is not the terminally ill friend, but the perfectly healthy relative who is killed in an accident. As my mother would say, "It is not always the leaning tree which falls first."

Not everything can be guaranteed forever, even if it should be. When I was tenured at Tulane, it meant that my teaching position could not be terminated. But in the aftermath of Hurricane Katrina, the engineering program was dropped

and I was out of a job overnight. The entire event brought back memories of my grandmother smoking her pipe and saying, "Baby, the only thing that is guaranteed is taxes and death!"

Not everything that looks new is new; most of it has been done before. Though parents now complain about sagging jeans on today's youth, we should remember that we did similar outlandish things when we were teens. Trends come and go; they often come back a little differently, but it's always the same thing as "there is nothing new under the sun."

If we look at those who have come before us, and the lessons they have passed down about life and reality, we will see that common sense is really one of our greatest tools in life. If "Hindsight is 20/20," then I need to know what those who have gone ahead of me have seen—that way, I can use their knowledge to create a new and successful reality for all.

You Can Tell a Zebra By his Stripes

*If it Looks Like a Duck,
Walks Like a Duck,
Quacks Like a Duck… It's a Duck.*

You really *can* tell a zebra by his stripes. The *Equus grevyi* zebra is larger than the plains zebra and has narrower and more plentiful black stripes. The mountain zebra, or *Equus zebra,* is smaller than the plains zebra and has no stripes on its belly. It's the same with birds: cardinals are red. The blackbird has distinctive markings. Look at their markings, and with the right reference, you can identify virtually any animal.

Humans are a bit more complicated, but the principle still holds. Your actions, or "markings," tell who you are. If I say that I care about you but then never call, what does that tell you? If you say you're dependable but you never come when you say you will, what am I supposed to think? In order to be thought of in a certain way, you must look that way, walk that way, act that way, and "quack" that way. And just as importantly, you must demand the same of those with whom you associate.

"Listen" to a person's actions, not their words. Only pay attention to their words to the extent that those words line up with their actions. It's easy to "sound" sincere, and many an individual has been duped by flowery speeches and protestations. You can tell a tree by the fruit it bears. When someone shows you who they are, believe them. Their stripes don't lie.

What do your "colors" say about you?

By their fruits shall ye know them.

Matthew 7:20

61

Oil & Water
Don't Mix

I'd like to turn this saying on its head. This piece of "wisdom" is actually questionable. It means to suggest that the rich ("oil") should not associate with the poor ("water").

Classism is one of those diseases—like racism and sexism—that pervades American culture. Classism is as American as apple pie or Chevrolet. So many individuals have been raised not to associate with people from a lower socioeconomic status. "Don't marry beneath your stature," your parents or grandparents may say. Or, on the other side, "Why are you marrying that 'hifalutin' boy (or girl)?" "You come from two different worlds," they may tell you. "It'll never work."

Let me invite you instead to consider the oil and water of people's hearts, rather than their purses. In the aftermath of Katrina, people returned to their homes to find everything destroyed. People were distraught as they drove around the city of New Orleans and there were no gas stations, no fast food establishments, no restaurants open. Electricity had been off since the hurricane hit and people were wondering where they might eat and get something to drink. People who never thought they would be in a Red Cross line or a church soup line found themselves standing there with everyone else. Hurricane Katrina, with all of her might and power, had mixed oil and water—the red bean lines included everyone, from the man with no money to the man with a million dollars in the bank, because neither had any choice. Money, wealth, and status didn't matter at that time… everyone was hungry and thirsty. In that moment, I am sure people judged each other much more by their compassion and their kindness than by their wallets or bank accounts.

Instruct those who are rich in this present world not to be conceited or to fix their hope on the uncertainty of riches, but on GOD, who richly supplies us with all things to enjoy.

1 Timothy 6:17 NASB

63

I have considered the days of old, the years of ancient times.

Psalm 77:5

Hindsight is 20/20 Vision

If we could go back in our lives, I am quite sure there are things that all of us would do differently. Many people say that they would not change anything about their lives. Well, knowing what I know now, I definitely would have purchased Microsoft's stock when the company went public. When we look back into the past we can see the mistakes and errors of our ways. Don't be discouraged about not having 20/20 vision until after the mistake; instead, commit to learning from the past and living a more prosperous future based on that hindsight. Hindsight is insight.

The devastating 2004 Indian Ocean tsunami killed approximately 300,000 people, but there was not a large-scale death of animals, and many wonder why. Some experts have speculated that the animals had a "sixth sense," or could hear acoustic waves from the earthquake that were inaudible to human beings. Consequently, while people were sunbathing on the beach, most of the animals headed for higher ground.

On the Surin Islands, 38 miles off the coast of Thailand, 196 members of a village survived the devastation that destroyed their village. When the tsunami wave hit Thailand, 5,300 people were killed. The Surin villagers remembered what they were taught by their ancestors: to run into the hills when God "eats the sea." The ancestors had 20/20 vision because they had seen it happen in the past. The villagers were in touch with their history through a living culture and, thus, they did not perish.

In 1965, Hurricane Betsy hit New Orleans and breached the levees in the Lower 9th Ward. Back then, black people were plucked off of rooftops by boats and helicopters. Forty years later, many of the children of those people plucked off of roofs found themselves in the same precarious position because they were not in touch with their history and culture, or simply chose not to act.

An Empty Wagon Makes the Most Noise

Content and information are very important, especially if you are faced with a presentation. It seems sometimes that the people who know the least are the loudest and most visible. If you are going to be loud and ostentatious, then you should make sure that everything you say or present is together and on point. You have to remove all doubt that your flamboyance is a defense mechanism to mask your ignorance, ineptness, or insecurity.

Due to the 24-hour news cycle, cable news stations are forced to fill every hour with some type of news or story. Therefore, any night you can turn on CNN, CNBC, or FOX News and see individuals who have mastered the ability to fill a silent void with unmitigated noise masquerading as knowledge and expertise. The individuals may very well be experts, but the format of the shows only allows for 30-second comments and responses to complex questions. Every presidential decision or political disagreement can't be solved or explained in a soundbite. Therefore, the news has been relegated to empty wagons making noise to get attention. Many of the guests have mastered the ability to make the most noise to get the most attention in the least amount of time. While the wagons on TV are actually subject experts most of the time, talk radio is a cornucopia of empty wagons making noise continuously to get ratings and attention. Individuals on talk radio—political, sports, religious, and societal—are usually put in positions to gather attention, regardless of their background. Talk radio is proof that the empty wagon makes the most noise. If you are going to speak, speak from a position of knowledge, facts, and expertise.

For a dream cometh through the multitude of business; and a fool's voice is known by multitude of words.

Ecclesiastes 5:3

Jesus said: "In a certain town there was a judge who neither feared GOD nor cared about men. And there was a widow in that town who kept coming to him with the plea, 'Grant me justice against my adversary.' For some time he refused. But finally he said to himself, 'Even though I don't fear GOD or care about men, yet because this widow keeps bothering me, I will see that she gets justice, so that she won't eventually wear me out with her coming!'"

Luke 18:2-5

A Squeaky Wheel Gets the Grease

Although the empty wagon makes the most noise, it is also true that the people who make the most noise are usually accommodated first and most. If you do not say anything, you definitely won't receive anything; if you say too much, you might meet the same fate. The trick is to walk the fine line between saying enough to get what you deserve and not being so docile that you are totally ignored. Walk carefully: sometimes the squeaky one or the most annoying one is also the first one shown the door!

Traveling a lot has taught me the meaning of service. When I am in a restaurant or hotel, there are certain expectations that I now have as I am paying for such service. Well, it is called the "Service Industry." When I feel that I have not received the service due me, I will go to all lengths to make sure that the establishment properly compensates me or immediately makes it right. I was taught by a wise person, "Never accept NO from a person who is not empowered to tell you YES." If my hotel room is not up to par or my food is not properly prepared, I will become the squeaky wheel until my needs (for which I paid) are met. I don't believe nor accept making noise for the sake of making noise, like harassing someone. I believe that one should fight for the service or their right due them.

69

Still Waters Run Deep

My mother always warned me that it is the quiet ones you have to worry about. When you look at a body of water and the surface is motionless, you know that the water is so deep that the current dissipates before it can influence the surface. Just like this still body of water, that quiet individual is the one who has internalized the issue, considered all the points, formulated a solution, and is waiting for the right moment to "bring down the house." Watch out for the calculated actions of the quiet ones; their words are few, but their actions can be most effective at creating tremendous good or tremendous evil.

And he said, Go forth, and stand upon the mount before the LORD. And, behold, the LORD passed by, and a great and strong wind rent the mountains, and broke in pieces the rocks before the LORD; but the LORD was not in the wind: and after the wind an earthquake; but the LORD was not in the earthquake: And after the earthquake a fire; but the LORD was not in the fire: and after the fire a still small voice.

1 Kings 19:11-13

The Calm Before the Storm

Our elders can always tell when a tornado is imminent. How? They look outside and see how calm the atmosphere is. If the air is stock still—no trees moving, no birds singing, no dogs barking—that's almost a sure sign that a tornado is coming.

This is an educational metaphor for us. It can sometimes be too quiet. When your children are in the house with you, and it gets quiet, you'd better go and check on them; they're probably into something. When your usually talkative friend, spouse, boss, or colleague turns quiet all of a sudden, be afraid... be very afraid. Many times, a period of quiet is followed by all heaven breaking loose!

> *The wise in heart shall be called prudent…*
>
> Proverbs 16:21

A Bird in the Hand is Worth Two in the Bush

One of the most popular game shows in history is "Let's Make a Deal," in which contestants usually won one prize by playing a game and then had to decide whether to trade that prize in for something unknown behind a glittering curtain. Do I keep what I have or risk it on something I don't even know about? Life often gives us the same decisions to make. I was often taught to go with the bird in the hand because you do not know what you might get by selecting the unknowns in the bush. They may fly away before you can catch them.

In other words, be prudent. When you look up the word prudent in the dictionary, the synonyms, or words with similar meanings, are careful and sensible. Be careful about throwing away something you already have for something of which you are not sure.

> Behold, I send you forth as sheep in the midst of wolves: be ye therefore wise as serpents, and harmless as doves.
>
> Matthew 10:16

Revenge is Best Served Cold

Don't Let the Right Hand Know What the Left One is Doing

I don't believe in revenge, but I do believe in protecting one's self, one's self-interest, and defending one's rights. Many times we find ourselves in situations where others are in control of our destiny, whether on a job or in school. Therefore, we can't always show our hand—we have to keep our cards, as people would say, close to our chest. When I have had to fight for an opportunity that I desire or one that I believe was unjustly denied, I did my best not to signal to my foe or judge my intentions. Strategy should be applied to all that you do and your plan should be your plan. If you were going after a contract for business, you wouldn't allow your competitor to read your proposal. Therefore, when you are defending or promoting yourself, you do not share the strategy with those who may not be in your corner. When it is necessary to challenge a report or evaluation, you want to present a sound, deliberate, and accurate case that catches everyone by surprise. You can rationalize anything, so you don't want to give those who may not be your supporter the time and opportunity to develop trumped-up responses to your issues or concerns. Serve them cold!

This is Where the Rubber Meets the Road

Sooner or later in our lives, there comes a time when we have to stop talking, take a stand, and do something. Many politicians and so-called leaders attempt to avoid controversy altogether. No one anymore wants to take a stand for what is right if it is unpopular. They would rather be popular, and see problems and issues persist, than lead. There are many issues that we are facing, from education to crime, unemployment to healthcare, and leaders need to address them head-on, honestly, and, most importantly, courageously. There are many issues, too, that you may have to meet head-on and show your beliefs and values through your actions, regardless of the consequences. When the rubber meets the road, where will you be? Because, for some people, the rubber never meets the road.

The Leaning Tree is not Always the One that Falls First

I have known many families with terminally ill members. The family usually comes together in a supportive and nurturing posture as the family member is making his or her transition. On more than one occasion, I have received a phone call with the shocking news of a family death which was not the one expected, not the one that was terminally ill. Death is never easy nor expected, so when you do expect an individual to die and someone else dies, it is like you are hit from the blind side. While struggling with this predicament, a wise person whom I greatly respect ended our conversation by saying, "It is not the leaning tree which always falls first." In essence, tomorrow isn't promised for anyone and the infirm should not be counted out too soon.

There is a time for everything, and a season for every activity under heaven: a time to be born and a time to die…

Ecclesiastes 3:1-2

Again, the kingdom of heaven is like a merchant looking for fine pearls. When he found one of great value, he went away and sold everything he had and bought it.

Matthew 13:45-46 NIV

One Man's Trash is Another Man's Treasure

Have you ever heard the phrase, "Whatever the market will bear?" That just means that the value of an item in the marketplace is directly related to what people are willing to spend/give up for that item. You might fall in love with and be willing to pay top dollar for an unusual house that very few others would want.

Which leads us to an even more important point: what exactly do you treasure? What is important to you? The answer to that question will determine and shape the course of your entire life. If you treasure money above all else, you will be subject to and at risk for unethical or illegal activity. If you treasure your family, you will be rewarded in ways you could never dream of. If you treasure your spirituality, you have achieved the pinnacle of living.

The Apple Doesn't Fall **Too Far** From the Tree

This is another ancient saying that represents an observation that is usually correct, but not always. It refers to the fact that children generally develop character and personality similar to their parents. Researchers tell us that even non-physical traits such as honesty, vulnerability to addiction, and personality, can at least in some part be attributed to genetics or parentage.

But environment and individual choice play a role as well. If you have/had good parents, great! Learn from them and reflect their best selves. If you didn't, don't worry—you always have a choice to do what's right. Here are two Bible verses that reflect this dual reality:

The person who sins will die. The son will not bear the punishment for the father's iniquity, nor will the father bear the punishment for the son's iniquity; the righteousness of the righteous will be upon himself, and the wickedness of the wicked will be upon himself.

Ezekiel 18:20

And he passed in front of Moses, proclaiming, "The LORD, the LORD, the compassionate and gracious GOD, slow to anger, abounding in love and faithfulness, maintaining love to thousands, and forgiving wickedness, rebellion and sin. Yet he does not leave the guilty unpunished; he punishes the children and their children for the sin of the parents to the third and fourth generation.

Exodus 34:6-7 NIV

You Can Tell the Tree By the Fruit That it Bears

The world is full of tragic stories of abuse by people who claimed to love the people they were abusing. A 20 year-old woman falls in love with a handsome young man, and finds that every "once in a while," he'll get violently angry. But it doesn't happen much, and he's so apologetic afterward that she ends up deciding he is "the one." After they get married, the abuse escalates. In too many cases, this woman ends up in the hospital or dead.

This statement is wisdom for the ages. "Fruit" is the acid test: the fruit of actions, that is. If someone is mean and hateful toward you, but claims that he or she loves you, believe their actions, not their words. Love is as love does. If they say they really want to work, but sleep in every day and rarely look for a job, believe their actions. The Bible says we are not to "judge," but that's not what this means. This isn't "judgment"; it's discernment. Let me put this another way: what you see is what you get. In essence, when someone shows you who they really are, believe them. A person will always show you their character, who they really are. All you have to do is discern it for what it is when you see it.

Beauty Is in the Eyes of the Beholder

A dress, a shoe, a color, an automobile, or a piece of furniture that is ugly to you may be very attractive to someone else. The beholder of these items, with his or her individual taste, determines the beauty. In essence, while beauty is only skin deep, it is also the prerogative of the one doing the judging. There is an old rhythm-and-blues song by Bill Withers called "Use Me" that says, "Brother if you only knew, you would wish you were in my shoes." Yes, we decide what beauty is, but we also have to take responsibility for our choices. When we, the beholder, decide to accept superficial skin-deep beauty, we as the beholder also accept the results of making such a decision. No one can determine or decide what beauty is for you; you have to live with your own determinations and decisions.

All of us have seen couples and wondered: "How did they get together? What attracted them to each other?" All of us have different preferences and needs to be met, so no one else can decide what is for you. Love is much deeper than what meets the eyes or the outer physical attributes of a person. If more people would decide what beauty is for themselves and then seek that out, we wouldn't have nearly as many family crises in this country.

So Jacob served seven years to get Rachel, but they seemed like only a few days to him because of his love for her.

Genesis 29:20 NIV

Now Saul feared David. It was clear that GOD was with David and had left Saul. So, Saul got David out of his sight by making him an officer in the army. David was in combat frequently. Everything David did turned out well. Yes, GOD was with him. As Saul saw David becoming more successful, he himself grew more fearful. He could see the handwriting on the wall.

1 Samuel 18:12-15 (The Message)

Every Good-bye Ain't Gone

Just because someone has left the building or your presence does not mean that his influence has departed. Some individuals come into our lives and impact our mind, body, and soul in ways that are detrimental to our well-being for years after they have physically departed. When we consider the number of single mothers and fatherless children in the world, this proverb comes to life. Many times in our life we will be faced with departures from friends, family members, and lovers, but just because someone said her farewell does not mean that she is gone forever. Even when the relationship or friendship ends on a sour note, the impact lingers like a faint perfume. And they "come back," at least in terms of their influence, at the most auspicious moments—like when you enter a new relationship, or when you try to get rid of someone, but they won't go away—at least in your mind.

Just look at this story about Israel's King Saul and David, God's chosen successor for him. Saul disobeyed God, and David "serendipitously" came to provide solace to Saul in the form of playing the harp. Then, when David killed Israel's enemy Goliath and the people turned their affections to him, Saul became jealous and tried to get David away from him by sending him into battle.

It didn't work, and Saul continued to be plagued by his jealousies.

Every good-bye ain't gone.

Pigs Don't Know Pigs Stink

If you ever had the blessing (or curse) of visiting a real rural pig's pen, you will never forget the aroma emanating from the pigs wallowing in six-inch-deep mud and slop. It's a smell, like smoke, which gets into your clothes and seems to follow you all your life. Well, the funny thing is that's the only smell that the pigs know, and they don't know it stinks. They play in it, roll around in it, and even eat in it. This is where and how they live.

Many people who have lived in one city or environment, worked for one company or manager, or never left their parents' home do not realize the limits of their environs. Not having ventured out, they do not know there is another way to live or work that just might be better. When you tell them what's not to love about their living environment, when you tell them about the limitations inherent in only experiencing one life or work or geography, it is you who is considered odd—just like telling a pig he stinks. As far as the pigs are concerned, you should join them in the pen!

It's amazing how rappers sing and glorify living in the "hood" or the ghetto. People used to work hard to get out of poverty and the ghetto, but now people are encouraging our youth to celebrate it and aspire to stay and never leave. Many of these rappers are now out of the pen and live in exclusive communities, but they still encourage others to remain in their squalor or the ghetto, like it is something wonderful and there is no place better, when all the time they have gotten out of the pen and are living in a better situation themselves. What hypocrisy! The youth buy into the hypocrisy because they have never seen anything different. They've never been out of the pen. Pigs don't know pigs stink!

> You say, "I am rich; I have acquired wealth and do not need a thing." But you do not realize that you are wretched, pitiful, poor, blind, and naked.
>
> Revelation 3:17

...your Father in heaven... causes his sun to rise on the evil and the good, and sends rain on the righteous and the unrighteous.

Matthew 5:45

God Watches Over Fools & Babies

Grandma's trying to tell us something here without being too harsh. She is giving some backhanded comfort as she assures you that, even though you may really be "messing up," God will have your back. He cares about you, and even when you act in ways contrary to His laws and principles, He will often step in and save you from yourself. Grandma, as has anyone who has lived long enough, has seen many situations in which a foolish action did not result in disastrous consequences.

Have you ever talked on your cell phone while driving on the freeway at 80 miles per hour? If you avoided an accident, you're a prime example of this proverb. Just look back and think about how many times you were spared from danger (despite your best efforts to step into it) and you will clearly understand the wisdom of this saying.

The subtle message, though, is this: even though God will watch over you, don't stay "out there" too long. There will be consequences.

In the Land of the Blind, a One-Eyed Man is King

A man's gift makes room for him, and brings him before great men.

Proverbs 18:16 NKJV

Grandma understood this truth: everything is relative. If you go into a work or organizational situation with a knowledge level that is significantly higher than the other individuals in the room, you will often find yourself being catered to and rewarded according to your wisdom. While you don't always want to be in a situation where you outstrip your colleagues by a few orders of magnitude, it is occasionally good to be in that position. It certainly helps your ego, but most importantly, it allows you an opportunity to be compensated according to your knowledge level. The key is to be a leading expert in one important area. Your particular talent, if you are able to use it to improve lives or institutions, is the key to your prosperity.

I have been involved in many grassroots campaigns and activities. As I grew and matured as a person and as a leader, I realized how important it is to come from a point of knowledge. Over the years, I have watched community activists and politicians knowingly provide incorrect information and deceptive answers to very complex questions. The activists or politicians usually get away with such responses because they are convinced that the audience is ignorant about the matter. Not very often does the community or audience get to challenge or question such comments. If everyone in the room is ignorant and you are the speaker, then the situation makes you an expert. The nation has to begin to expect more out of our leaders at all levels. As we move deeper into the 21st century where technology is placing more and more information at people's fingertips instantly, the one-eyed man can't get away with taking advantage of the people's ignorance much longer.

If you Throw a **Brick**
in a Pack of Dogs,
the Only One that
Howls
is the One that was **Hit**

*A hit dog
will holler!*

Speaking to an audience once, I made some general but pointed allegations about the state of the United States and clergy leaders. No one in the audience dared challenge the assertions, for they were factual and on point. It did seem, however, to be difficult for the audience to receive the facts as presented. Sometimes soul-searching reveals more than we are willing to deal with. One lady approached—or should I say confronted—me and stated, "I don't appreciate you talking about my pastor." I responded, "Miss, with all due respect, I didn't say anything about your pastor; I was speaking in general... so if I threw a brick in a pack of dogs, the only one that howls is the one that was hit." She recognized the truth for herself because the facts fit her situation. Her pastor was guilty of the transgressions that I outlined... so it seemed to her that the entire presentation was about him. The brick hit her!

You know when you've hit a nerve. To paraphrase a very famous lawyer's line, "If it doesn't fit, you must acquit—yourself." But oh, if it does, you're hit; and when you're hit, I challenge you to go beyond hollering and take out some time for a serious self-critique.

There is a biblical story that illustrates this in a powerful way. King David, as many of you know, was king of Israel, and he had a wandering eye. He looked upon the form of a beautiful woman, Bathsheba, and immediately summoned her to his castle for an extramarital tryst (they were both married). When she announced that she was pregnant, he sent her husband to the front lines of a war that Israel was fighting, to his certain death, so that he could marry her and cover up his infidelity. His spiritual advisor, Nathan, however, discovered his sin and came to him with a parable that precisely fit what David had done. "What if a rich man had many sheep and decided to steal one lamb from a poor man?" Nathan asked him. Immediately, David took umbrage and called for the man to be severely punished. He was hit! Nathan waited for the story to sink in, and then gave the zinger: "You are that man," he told David. Hit again! Consider David's response, seen in the passage to the right. If you ever become a "hit dog," take a page out of his book.

For I acknowledge my transgressions, and my sin is always before me... Create in me a clean heart, O GOD, and renew a steadfast spirit within me.

Psalm 51:3, 10

There Are Only
Two Guarantees
in Life: Death & Taxes

In the world that we now live in, people are always promising many things. Many of us think that a degree will guarantee us some security in life. We believe that we are in total control of this thing called life. But life has a way of teaching you who is actually in control. I always dreamed of becoming and receiving tenure from a major research university. I eventually received tenure at Tulane University at the age of 35 and people told me that I was set for life, because you can't get fired with tenure. You have a guaranteed job for life. Guaranteed!

Well, God had a different plan, and in the aftermath of Katrina, Tulane decided to eliminate its engineering program due to financial exigency. My guaranteed six-figure job was gone. There are no guarantees in life that man can make to us. People are convinced that they will pay taxes until they die, so the cliché is that the only two guarantees are death and taxes. All of us were born the same way, through a gush of blood and water, which started our trek toward the inevitable, death. Nothing, and I mean nothing, other than that is guaranteed. Not even taxes!

And he told them this parable: "The ground of a certain rich man produced a good crop. He thought to himself, 'What shall I do? I have no place to store my crops.' Then he said, 'This is what I'll do. I will tear down my barns and build bigger ones, and there I will store all my grain and my goods. And I'll say to myself, "You have plenty of good things laid up for many years. Take life easy; eat, drink and be merry."' But GOD said to him, 'You fool! This very night your life will be demanded from you.'"

Luke 12:16-20

That is Too Much Like Right

Some people will not do what they know to be right to save their lives. You can coach, teach, educate, direct, and mentor them and they still mess it all up. Often when my siblings and I would do something bad (and my mother knew she had taught us differently), she would say we wouldn't be good because "that would be too much like right." In other words, we were bent on doing wrong for the sake of doing wrong. Innately, humans know what is right and how to treat each other, but simply just refuse to do the right thing. When responding to some previous hurt by someone, many of us go out of our way to avoid doing what we should do to treat each other well. I guess it would be too much like right. Many times you will loan people money and they will agree to pay you back at some specified time or within some timeframe. Then you see them after that date or period and they haven't paid you, but they are sporting a new car or clothes or have something that cost more than what they owed you. It becomes clear to you that the individual has made a conscious choice to not do what is right and repay his debt to you. Paying you the money they owe you would be too much like right!

You Don't Have to Trouble **Trouble** For Trouble to **Trouble You**

There are days when it appears as if trouble has its mark on you. Every way you turn, trouble lurks. Despite your best intentions of avoiding conflict and confrontation, it manages to find you like a laser-guided missile. When trouble finds you, it is good to understand that you are not always responsible for its arrival, but you are responsible for its departure or minimization. Do not make a bad situation worse by losing your cool or temper. Handle the situation even if you are not responsible for it and move on.

Neither I nor my fellow residents of the Gulf Coast asked for the troubles and problems of Hurricane Katrina. Similarly, there have been times I left my house just to take a relaxing ride and the police pulled me over for nothing. I hadn't broken the law but the police were troubling me for no reason. You don't have to trouble trouble for trouble to trouble you, so prepare yourself mentally, physically, and spiritually for when the trouble comes… for it is coming!

Man is born to trouble…

Job 5:7 NIV

...there is
no new thing
under the sun.

Ecclesiastes 1:9

There's Nothing New Under the Sun

Every couple of years people reinvent a way to recast the Ponzi pyramid scheme, which eventually swindles unsuspecting people out of millions of dollars. Many multiple-level marketing programs change their names every ten years and get some of the same people. As we study history and many of the so-called creative movies, inventions, dances, and schemes of today, we realize that they are just different takes on things of the past. The games men run on women were the same games of fifty years ago. That's why it seems like your mother is always right, because she knows the outcome to a situation before it has run its course. She had seen it before in her lifetime.

Even today, I watch as kids drive adults crazy by the way they dress. The sagging pants and the showing of their underwear just seems so classless and disrespectful. Many of us in my generation act as if we didn't do anything like that; however, if we shut our eyes and think long and honestly, we have to say that we came close. All of these kids call each other "dog," while we called each other "cat." We wore our Levi jeans around our waist, but we pulled our boxer undershorts out of our pants for all to see. We wore Hushpuppies shoes and brushed them more than we brushed our teeth and dared anyone to step on them. There is truly nothing new under the sun.

Relationships

One of the most important parts of who you become is the people with whom you choose to surround yourself. We encounter many different types of relationships throughout our lives, but each plays a crucial role in who we are and how others perceive us.

Be careful how you act around children, especially your own. My sons look up to me, no matter what I am doing, and they constantly mimic my behavior. I must try every day to set a good example for them because "they may not do as I say, but will definitely do as I do."

Be careful whom you choose as your friends. As a child, I had the opportunity to associate with boys who were always getting into trouble, but I chose to avoid them so that others would not see me in the same light. Often, people who make trouble will bring their friends along with them, because as we know, "misery loves company."

The road you walk alone is very, very, very long.

How do you create healthy and meaningful relationships?

Be careful how you treat your enemies; though good relationships are essential, you should know who your enemies are as well. While at Tulane, many professors resented my young age and swagger. Instead of keeping to myself, I tried to be around my enemies often; when an attack eventually came, I was able to see it coming and prevent it from doing any damage.

Everyone you encounter will impact you in some way. It is up to you to decide how you will respond. Seek to have mutually beneficial and genuine relationships with everyone. Authenticity is the glue to creating meaningful relationships.

Shared joy is a double joy; shared sorrow is half a sorrow.

Swedish Proverb

Cows Know When To Go Home

It is said that guests will bring you joy either by arriving or departing. Some people wear out their welcome when visiting you. Cows actually begin their trek home as the sun begins to set. We should take lessons from the cow. Haven't you ever had the experience where someone drops by and stays past "bedtime?" You yawn, you sigh, you might even say, "Boy it's getting late," but they just don't get the hint.

Leave your host's home at a respectable time. Do not overstay your welcome.

It was hard to find a verse for this one. So, all you Bible scholars, don't be mad; I know this verse is taken out of context…

You Can Do
Bad
All by Yourself

Life is tough enough, so we do not need to surround ourselves with individuals who will add challenges to our experiences on this earth. My mother was adamant about who she allowed in her life for this very reason. She would admonish her children, especially her daughters, with this proverb. Many relationships would be better off if the parties would have mastered this proverb first. Bring people into your life who will help you move forward from where you are presently; eliminate those individuals today who have a negative impact on your life.

The NFL star quarterback Michael Vick lost a $100 million contract and spent nearly two years in federal prison for his actions and those of his associates. Vick had everything to lose by hanging around shady characters, and the characters had everything to gain and nothing to lose. By associating with people with so much risk, Vick knowingly placed himself in an environment that eventually destroyed him. He could have done bad all by himself, but he chose to get some help. He was not the first, and sadly it seems he won't be the last, as many entertainers, athletic stars, and other celebrities continue to run with people who mean them no good. We can see them and judge them, but those of us not in the media spotlight also need to determine the necessity of the people who are around us. What kind of company do you keep?

> Do not be misled: "Bad company corrupts good character."
>
> I Corinthians 15:33

...you do not
know what
a day may
bring forth.

Proverbs 27:1 NIV

Give Me My Flowers While I am Living

Many individuals live life complaining and whining about the people in their lives rather than appreciating them. We take each other for granted as if nothing will change and all of us will be here forever.

My mother made her transition at the young and tender age of fifty-one. I honestly feel that she gave her life so that her children could have one, continuously sacrificing so that we could have what we needed. If we needed clothes, shoes, food, or pocket money, she somehow found a way to provide it. She would often tell me to give her flowers while she was living, for "dead people cannot smell."

Start thinking of every individual with whom you have a relationship—whether romantic, platonic, or professional—as a "teacher" who is in your life for a reason and specifically designated to provide you with a lesson. These teachers will guide and direct you in ways that you probably will not understand until much later. Usually the only problem is that the "teacher" is no longer there or available for you to shower them with praise. As life continues to throw you curve balls, you will reflect on the teacher that you did not appreciate when you were receiving the valuable lessons. That is why it is important to show everyone appreciation and love daily. I often wish I had observed the lessons while they were being taught; instead, I was usually too busy focusing on the future. Don't be that way. Say "thank you," "I am sorry," "I forgive you," and "please forgive me" because tomorrow may be too late.

Don't Bite the Hand that Feeds You

Humans have a habit of hurting those closest to us. We should be most gentle with those around us who support us and help us to be the individuals that we are. Your parents, friends, employers, and clients are some of the hands that provide sustenance for you to exist. We should tread carefully and lightly when challenging these individuals. Definitely stand by your principles and be willing to sever any relationship that does not serve your best interests; however, do not pick fights for the sake of fighting, especially with those who "feed" you. Sometimes we just have to eat humble pie!

Take a clue from King David of the Bible. He was clearly anointed by God to be Israel's second king after Saul, but first he found himself in a subservient position to Saul. Saul became jealous because David won the hearts of the people, and at various times tried and conspired to kill David. David had an opportunity at one point to kill Saul in a vulnerable moment when Saul lay sleeping. Here is what he did with that opportunity, and what he said about it:

So David and Abishai went to the army by night, and there was Saul, lying asleep inside the camp with his spear stuck in the ground near his head. Abner and the soldiers were lying around him. Abishai said to David, "Today GOD has delivered your enemy into your hands. Now let me pin him to the ground with one thrust of my spear; I won't strike him twice." But David said to Abishai, "Don't destroy him! Who can lay a hand on the LORD's anointed and be guiltless? As surely as the LORD lives," he said, "the LORD himself will strike him; either his time will come and he will die, or he will go into battle and perish. But the LORD forbid that I should lay a hand on the LORD's anointed. Now get the spear and water jug that are near his head, and let's go."

I Samuel 26:7-11

My son, if sinners entice you, do not give in to them. If they say, "Come along with us; let's lie in wait for someone's blood, let's waylay some harmless soul; let's swallow them alive, like the grave, and whole, like those who go down to the pit; we will get all sorts of valuable things and fill our houses with plunder; throw in your lot with us, and we will share a common purse." My son, do not go along with them, do not set foot on their paths; for their feet rush into sin, they are swift to shed blood.

Proverbs 1:10-16

Misery Loves Company

No one wants to be alone, especially if they are doing wrong. When I would plot to carry out some devilment in the neighborhood or at school, I would always first find an accomplice. If I got caught, I did not want to be the only one going to the principal's office or to jail or to get a spanking; therefore, I would recruit everyone I could find to participate in my schemes just in case. My mother would often tell me to be aware of my friends who were not doing well or stayed in trouble because they may not want to be "the only one." When in trouble I would often say, "My friends did it too," or, "They made me do it," and she would respond, "Don't you know that misery loves company?" Over the years I have learned that it really does, and that's why I take personal responsibility for my actions.

It seems that youth never get into trouble by themselves. We always see two or more youth arrested for some heinous crime or mischief—like it took all of them to think of this crazy failed plan that resulted in their arrest. When we dig deeper, we find that it was usually one who recruited the rest and convinced them to follow. The leader did it because he didn't want to be alone; he wanted others to share in his misery. When misery comes knocking, you better pray for the discernment necessary to see it. And remember: it can come from friends, family, or foes.

If You Lay Down with Dogs, You'll Get Up with Fleas

For some reason, this was my mother's favorite proverb. She would recite this one incessantly whenever I shared with her stories about individuals who were going to help me. She would indicate that you do not want to associate with everyone, for their baggage will be your baggage in the end. Many unsavory characters show up when you are doing great things, offering you money, clothes, and other goodies.

Just think of all the high school athletic "phenoms." They are heavily recruited and fêted by alums, but also by unsavory characters who offer them money, cars, and jobs "under the table." Then later, the information leaks out, and those associations end up tainting the reputation of the athlete, the school they attended, and ultimately even their associates and friends. Those are the kinds of "dogs" to avoid, and their example is applicable to anyone. Whether in sports, in the professions, in business, or in life, keep away from people with bad reputations and poor character, or society will paint you with the same broad brush.

That kind of persuasion does not come from the one who calls you. "A little yeast works through the whole batch of dough."

Galatians 5:8-9

One Bad Apple Can Ruin the Entire Sack

The thing about cancer is that when it is detected, the doctors immediately begin a treatment regimen or surgery to remove it. The doctor knows that a cancer untreated will bring certain death to the patient. The cancerous cells and organs must be contained and then eliminated.

In life and business when we discover a cancer or a bad apple, we must immediately begin the process of eradicating it out of our lives and organizations. This one bad apple will begin to spread like a cancer, poisoning our lives, outlook, mission, vision, and purpose. It only takes one bad cancer cell to start the deterioration. We are talking about that cancerous employee, coworker, team member, or friend. Such examples are visible throughout the sports world.

One who comes to mind is the football player Terrell Owens, formerly of the San Francisco 49ers, Philadelphia Eagles, and Dallas Cowboys. It is clear that wherever he goes, he has been a problem for the team and its chemistry. When someone with so much talent continues to move (or be moved), it implies that something is wrong and the organizations have come to the painful realization that the team would be better without this individual. They sacrifice this one person to save the team. Look around you; there may be some individuals you need to remove from your life so that you can do better.

Birds
of a Feather
Flock
Together

People with similar characteristics usually hang together. If your friend is a criminal, then you are. Rightly or wrongly, people judge you on your associations. I had some friends in the neighborhood who often caused trouble for the community and were not doing well in school. I had to make a choice not to hang with them because people began to make judgments about me based on my relationship with them. I had to be very careful about what I did with them and when I was seen with them. I did not need or want my reputation tainted by hanging with the flock.

The Book of Daniel provides a great example of some young men who "hung" together under the most threatening of circumstances. You probably recognize their names if you ever went to Sunday School: Shadrach, Meshach, and Abednego, the three Hebrew boys threatened with death for refusing to bow down and worship the king. "We only bow down to God," they said. (See also page 192.)

Iron
Sharpens
—— iron

> *As iron sharpens iron, so one man sharpens another.*
>
> Proverbs 27:17

We have to be careful about the individuals with whom we find ourselves associating. You want to be around people whose character, purpose, and direction is similar to yours, for these individuals will only make you better. The people in your circle should challenge you and help you to grow into the human being or professional you want to be. If you're "iron"—that is, if you're thinking progressively and constructively about your purpose and the course of your life—you don't want to hang out with "wood", or people who aren't doing that. That is why many a time we say that "birds of a feather flock together," or, as Grandma said, "Show me your friends and I'll show you who you are." Your flock of friends will have a dominant characteristic that will eventually influence who you become.

Listen, friends, to some fatherly advice; sit up and take notice so you'll know how to live.

Proverbs 4:1

125

A Minute of Passion Can Cause a Lifetime of Pain

Keep Your Skirt Down and Your Legs Crossed

Do I really need to explain this? Young ladies, be very careful about your sexual involvements. Your sexuality is a precious gift and not one to spread around indiscriminately. It might seem old-fashioned, but Grandma really did know what she was talking about. You probably already know about the risks of sexually transmitted diseases like AIDS, and now the widespread prevalence among men and women of HPV (Human Papilloma Virus) that can lead to cervical cancer in women. Do you also know about the emotional risks and risks to your future of many and varied sexual liaisons? Do you know that a sexual relationship can make you think the wrong one is "Mr. or Mrs. Right"? Do you understand the emotional and spiritual connection that takes place, and how difficult it is to break? Even more importantly, do you understand that it is the nature of the male species to hunt, and if he can capture without having to make a commitment, that's just fine with him?

My advice to you young men is similar. Young ladies these days are more and more sexually aggressive, and you will need to keep your wits about you to ensure that you stay emotionally and physically healthy and able to ultimately engage in a mature, committed relationship. You can fall into the same trap, thinking the young lady who pursues and "overtakes" you is "the one."

This advice is designed not to keep you from having fun, but to protect you. Heed it, and you'll find a much easier, emotionally balanced life—and much joy when you finally find "the one," minus the baggage!

Flee fornication.

1 Corinthians 6:18 KJV

I Brought You **Into** & This World I'll Take You **Out**

Do you remember this proverb? You may not; that parental threat has kind of gone out of favor, with the growing attention paid to child abuse. Of course parents and grandmothers didn't literally mean it! But what's the point here? The point is that what they were focusing on was the "I brought you into this world" part. Parents are responsible, according to God, for the wise upbringing of their children and will go to great lengths to ensure that they "turn out alright." Even if it means punishment, or even if it means instituting consequences that are very painful (emotionally and, yes, sometimes physically—but not to the point of abuse) for the child. Here's the translation: "I brought you into this world and by God, you are going to be a responsible, God-fearing human being—I'll see to that!" That's something to be grateful for.

Now a word to parents: it is cruel to punish a child for something they have done when they have not been taught right from wrong. It is a parent's responsibility to model their children's lives. You mold clay; clay does not decide how it is formed. However, even if we don't mold the clay, it still takes on a shape. Many of the issues we are seeing with youth today are caused by people not having taken the time to mold the clay. They have not behaved responsibly regarding their children. You created it; now, shape it for good and you may never have to invoke this proverb.

Train up a child in the way he should go: and when he is old, he will not depart from it.

Proverbs 22:6

You Catch More Flies with Honey than with Vinegar

Supervisors are often guilty of this: demanding that their employees perform by using "sticks" such as the threat of dismissal, salary cutbacks, or some other sanction. Human resources experts will tell you that this method simply doesn't work. People are motivated by the positive, not the negative. Offering them an incentive that they truly value is what gets people motivated. It's the same in non-work life. How do you talk to the people closest to you? Do you complain, and yell, and moan to get things done around the house, or at church or school?

Consider Abigail, a figure in the Old Testament. She was married to a real jerk named Nabal. David was not yet king at the time, but Abigail knew that he would be someday. David was traveling the countryside and sent his servants to ask Nabal for food and provisions for their journey. Nabal sent back a cryptic message that essentially told him to "stick it." Angered, David planned to kill Nabal and his men. Fortunately for him, Nabal had a wise wife:

"…let this gift, which your servant has brought to my master, be given to the men who follow you. Please forgive your servant's offense… Let no wrongdoing be found in you as long as you live… When the LORD has done for my master every good thing he promised concerning him and has appointed him leader over Israel, my master will not have on his conscience the staggering burden of needless bloodshed or of having avenged himself. And when the LORD has brought my master success, remember your servant."

I Samuel 25:27-31

Abigail's kind and solicitous words saved Nabal's life.
Incidentally, when Nabal died, David asked Abigail to marry him!

130

It's Not
What You
Say But How
You Say It

Don't Call a
Dog with
a Stick in
Your Hand

Keep Your Friends Close, & Your Enemies Closer

> But love your enemies, do good to them, and lend to them without expecting to get anything back. Then your reward will be great, and you will be sons of the Most High, because he is kind to the ungrateful and wicked.
>
> Luke 6:35 NIV

You may remember this line from the movie "The Godfather." It is attributed to the brilliant Chinese general and military strategist Sun Tzu, circa 400 B.C. What does it mean? Your friends are naturally close, but to be safe, you need to know what your enemies are doing and how they're thinking—so, stay close to them. Got an enemy at work? Have lunch with them. Talk to them frequently. Do favors for them, even. Get to know their moods, moves, and mannerisms. It keeps them off-guard; it can even keep them from thinking of you as an enemy. And one day, you may catch them in an unguarded moment and uncover their real intentions. Or... you may just make a friend.

As a professor fresh out of college, I took my first job at a prestigious university. I was so elated that I had finally achieved my dream of becoming a university faculty member. Every day as I showed up to work and attended faculty meetings, it became clear that many of my colleagues were not too happy about my presence. Daily they did things to sabotage my efforts or deflect from my achievements. It would have been easy for me to separate from them and stay in my office, but I had to keep my enemies close so that I could witness their strategy and learn their motives. That way I was able to plot and prepare for their ultimate attack. When they finally did attack, I was prepared, they failed, and I am still standing. Keep your known enemies closer than you keep your friends.

Love is as Love Does

> Suppose a brother or sister is without clothes and daily food. If one of you says to him, "Go, I wish you well; keep warm and well fed," but does nothing about his physical needs, what good is it?
>
> James 2:15-16

Hurricane Katrina devastated the Gulf Coast of the U.S. and New Orleans on August 29, 2005. Almost one year later after the storm, nearly 70% of the House of Representatives and 45% of the Senate had not visited the city of New Orleans according to Women of the Storm, a non-partisan alliance of women in Louisiana whose families, friends, businesses, or lives were impacted by Hurricanes Katrina or Rita (www.womenofthestorm.org). How could close to 75% of the 535 leaders of this country choose not to visit the worst man-made, natural disaster in the history of this country? How could they claim they love this country when their actions show differently?

Love is as love does. Love can be shown in words, but it is the actions that give power to those words. With one half million of their fellow Americans homeless, helpless, hungry, thirsty, overwhelmed, and depressed, they chose to stay away. How can that be love? How can that be compassion? In contrast to firefighters who run to burning buildings, thus showing their compassion, love, and bravery, these leaders stayed away, showing their cowardice, lack of concern, and indifference, which is definitely not what love would have done.

Children
May Not Do as You Say
But They Will Definitely
Do as You Do

*...and parents
are the pride of
their children.*

Proverbs 17:6

I have two sons and it is absolutely unbelievable how they watch what I do. My oldest son mimics my every move. When watching the football or basketball game, I scream "Ooooh." He can be playing with his toys, but he screams "Ooooh," too. When I drink water and then say satisfactorily, "Aaaah," he runs up to me, drinks, and says "Aaaah," too. Therefore, if I curse and disrespect his mother or other women, he will do that also. Parents and adults are their children's first teachers and should always be cognizant of that, in and out of their presence. We have to develop personable and good habits because we never know who is watching us.

...follow my example...

I Corinthians 11:1 NIV

Morals & Mouth

How Must You Conduct Yourself in a Moral Universe?

Though you cannot control the actions and words of others, you can control your own. Having a strong moral base—both in deed and in words—is essential to your personal integrity.

It is important to stand up for what you believe in, no matter what others are saying. My entire life, I have had to go against what other people were saying in order to achieve my dreams and do what I knew was right.

It is important to keep your promises. After guaranteeing a young girl that I would send her a copy of my first book, she was shocked when I actually followed through. So many adults had let her down that it was important for me to show her that some people really do keep their word.

It is important to consider the consequences of what you say to others. Though many people believe it to be "sour grapes" when I criticize Tulane because of the loss of my tenured position and closing of its

How Does What You Say Affect How You Live?

engineering school, or the President and federal government for its poor response to the hurricane disaster, I know that I was speaking truth to power (which is the essence of a democracy). Theodore Roosevelt, the 26th President of the United States, once stated, "To announce that there must be no criticism of the President, or that we are to stand by the President, right or wrong, is not only unpatriotic and servile, but is morally treasonable to the American public. Nothing but the truth should be spoken about him or any one else." The truth is never sour grapes.

Knowing who you are and what you stand for is a key piece of moral integrity, and it is essential to maintain your morality in what you say and do. The impeccability of your word is the essence of who you are and how you will be perceived. Always let the truth come out of your mouth.

If it's Good for the Goose It's Good for the Gander

When Jesse Jackson ran for president in 1984, I'll never forget a *Time* magazine cover that read, "What does Jesse want?" When the question was posed to Rev. Jackson he answered with the quip, "I want to be the President of the United States of America. If other people believe they can be president, why can't I, an African American in a free country?" If a policy, advantage, or privilege has worked and sustained one person, then it should work and sustain others also. In America we have selective amnesia about how certain individuals have, and continue to benefit from, privilege and advantage, and those same individuals are the ones who will protest the loudest when the same opportunities are afforded to others. If it was good enough for them, then it is good enough for everyone.

In 1954, the U.S. Supreme Court ruled that "separate but unequal" Jim Crow segregation laws were unconstitutional. All children deserved and still deserve equal access to a quality education. Still, today, we see that, for many, this principle set down by our highest legal authorities is still not reality. At prestigious universities, we watch annually as children of privilege and wealth are admitted regardless of their academic record, but students who have worked hard and even achieved more are turned away!

> If you show special attention to the man wearing fine clothes and say, "Here's a good seat for you," but say to the poor man, "You stand there" or "Sit on the floor by my feet," have you not discriminated among yourselves and become judges with evil thoughts?
>
> James 2:3-4

A Half-Truth is a Whole Lie

If Someone Would Lie, They Would Steal; And If Someone Would Steal, They Would Kill.

People often think in terms of "little" sins and "big" sins. Telling a "white lie" is OK; murder is not. But these proverbs suggest that there is a slippery slope down which you should not even start to fall. We all fall; we all stumble. But be careful if it gets a little too easy to break one of the Ten Commandments, or your parents' commandments, or the civil law. Grandma is telling us here how to examine and judge the character of an individual. We have to be careful, Grandma teaches us, of the person who would lie to you, for they may do other things as well. And be careful lest you go down that slippery slope as well.

One of the most tragic examples of this is found in the Old Testament story of David. You probably know the story, but have you ever thought about this? David's sin began when he desired another man's wife, Bathsheba. That was the sin of lust.

Then, he acted on that lust by summoning her to his castle for a clandestine affair—lust became adultery. Then, when he found out that she was pregnant, he summoned her husband, who was part of his military contingent, home so that he could spend time with his wife and cover up the true paternity of the child. That's deception, otherwise known as lying. Finally, when the husband refused to sleep with his wife out of a loyal commitment to his king (David), David sent him back out to the front lines of battle to make sure he would be killed. That's murder. So lust became adultery, which became deception, which became murder. David paid dearly for that slippery slope. The guilt nearly consumed him, and he and Bathsheba, though they ultimately married, lost their first child. It's not worth going down that road.

For whoever keeps the whole law and yet stumbles at just one point is guilty of breaking all of it.

James 2:10 NIV

Seest thou a
man diligent in
his business?
He shall stand
before kings; he
shall not stand
before mean
men.

Proverbs 22:29

An Ounce of
Discipline
is Worth a Pound of **prayer**

Prayer is important; Grandma would never say that it wasn't. But the singular act of praying cannot be viewed in isolation. It does no good to pray if you aren't willing to do what is necessary to live a good life. You can't sleep late and fool around before a test and then ask God to bless your efforts.

"I'm blessed" is a response you hear from a lot of individuals today in response to the question "How are you doing?" I look around and people are praying about everyone and everything. As a Christian, I believe and advocate prayer, but I also know that many prayers would not be necessary if we were more disciplined.

If we followed the scripture and feared the wrath of the Lord, there would be many prayers that would never need to be prayed.

Live your life accordingly and avoid many of the pitfalls that come with being disobedient. I'm not pointing the finger; I too have prayed prayers that had to be prayed because I wasn't doing what I was supposed to be doing, especially when it came to my physical health. Many of us find ourselves in compromising positions of poor health or financial distress because we were not disciplined. We find ourselves praying to be delivered from all these bills and poor health, both of which might have been avoided if we ate better, exercised regularly, and didn't spend frivolously. If we would get some structure and order in our lives, there would be some prayers we wouldn't have to pray.

An **Idle Mind** is a **Devil's** workshop

Grandma hated "idleness," a word that has fallen out of favor of late. It was an idea with long-standing roots: "slothfulness," or laziness, was considered one of the chief sins. People with a lot of idle time get bored easily and are therefore more likely to fall into trouble. Why are people idle? Because they don't have goals, they're not striving for something.

There are so many things to do, so many places to visit, and so much information to learn! Life is a banquet feast of possibilities. If you see life that way, you can never be bored, and you'll always have something to do.

Occupy till I come.

Luke 19:13

The hand of the diligent will rule, while the slothful will be put to forced labor.

Proverbs 12:24

147

A Dead Fish Can Go with the Flow, But it Takes a Mighty Strong One to Go Against It

John F. Kennedy stated that conformity is the death of freedom and the destroyer of creativity. America is a nation where its citizens are supposed to be free; but there are nonetheless strong competing forces enticing us to conform and be like others. We were born to be free, especially living in the most "liberated" nation on earth. Sadly, many people wake up every day in this free nation and decide to live in the cage that others have built for them. Why do they do it? They fail to develop the muscles needed to go against the prevailing wave of conformity. One can be literally near death and follow the crowd, but it takes intestinal fortitude to do your own thing and create what has never been created or achieve what has never been achieved. That's the promise of humanity. I challenge you to be among the few who go against the flow.

All my life I have gone against the flow of prevailing attitudes in order to achieve the things that I have. Your family, friends, and society try to force you to conform to what they think or want for you.

Stand. Develop the strength. Follow your heart, even if it's against the wishes of others. In the end, you'll be happy, even if you miss the mark, because you will have tried to make your dreams come into reality, something most of the world will never be able to claim!

But small is the gate and narrow the road that leads to life, and only a few find it.

Matthew 7:14

Two Wrongs Don't Make a Right

Don't Cut Off Your Nose to Spite Your Face

Not all old sayings are valid. One example: revenge is never sweet. Researchers have now confirmed that revenge actually damages your health. The possible consequences—elevated blood pressure, ulcers, headaches—are just not worth the very temporary satisfaction of angrily repaying people in kind for hurting you. I'm not talking about seeking remedies for grievances through officially sanctioned means such as the courts. I'm talking about the scheming that some people do to "get back" at someone in a vindictive and hurtful way.

Grandma would be nonplussed by the research about the dangerous health consequences of a vengeful attitude. She's been telling us that for years. And she didn't need mountains of studies, tests, and statistics. She had the wisdom of experience. A dark room is only illuminated with light; so is the dark heart. You must be the light in the dark world. As the motto of my alma mater translates from Latin, "Don't curse the darkness, light a candle."

> Do not repay anyone evil for evil... overcome evil with good.
>
> Romans 12:17, 21

150

You Don't Have a Pot to Pee in and a Window to Throw it Out of

Whenever I thought I was smarter than my elders, this proverb was their classic comeback. I would bravely and aggressively offer my opinions about life, or assert what I would or would not do, or make a critique, and they would always be able to take me down a peg or two with that acerbic retort. Here was the point: if I don't have an independent way to take care of myself, I really don't have much to say that would impress any of my elders. It sounds harsh, but I got the message. Now, I have the pot, the window... and the house to go with it.

> If anyone thinks he is something when he is nothing, he deceives himself.
>
> — Galatians 6:3

151

Your Word is Your Bond

Your Word is the Only Thing You Have

Nothing is more important than the word. Words spoke the world into existence. Words have started wars and ushered in peace. Words kill and heal, bond and break relationships.

Your word must be good. If it's not, you can't be trusted for anything. If you say you're going to do something, do it. If you talk about something that happened, tell the truth. People who can be trusted to follow through, no matter what it costs them, are gold in the marketplace—of work and business, and of personal relationships.

Recently, after speaking to a group of wayward youth at a group home, a young lady asked me for a copy of my book, *A View From the Roof.* I told her that I didn't have a copy with me but if she emailed me I would send her one. Two days later I received an email requesting a book but with no postal mailing address. After I responded asking her for a mailing address, she responded, "Wow, I guess there are adults you can believe in." What she was really saying is that she was impressed that she had met someone with an impeccable word. Obviously, the word of others had rung hollow so often, she began to believe that was the norm. Too many people have lied to their children and not stood by their word, with the unfortunate result that children generally do not believe in adults anymore.

152

LORD, who may dwell in your sanctuary? Who may live on your holy hill? He... who speaks the truth from his heart and... who keeps his oath even when it hurts... He who does these things will never be shaken.

Psalm 15:1-2, 4

Loose Lips Sink Ships

A fish can't get caught with his mouth closed

There is a reason why, in 1966, the U.S. Supreme Court decided that persons arrested by law enforcement authorities would automatically and explicitly have "the right to remain silent." Your words can incriminate you. They can be used against you. A good attorney can compare a statement you made in January with another statement you made in June and find inconsistencies and contradictions that the average layperson would never find. And the more words that can be attributed to you, the greater the chance that your words can be used against you.

If you're in a troubled situation, if you find yourself accused of some wrongdoing, or if you find your integrity compromised, remember this: the fewer your words, the better. In essence, when you are under attack or in the presence of hostility, it is better to remain quiet until you can collect your facts and properly defend yourself.

It's Better to Remain Quiet and Be Thought of as a Fool,

> A fool uttereth all his mind: but a wise man keepeth it in till afterwards.
>
> Proverbs 29:11

If you have begun your foray into the world of work, you may have noticed something. There are people who talk all the time, and there are people who don't talk all the time. The longer you work, the more you will notice something else: the people who talk all the time are generally not as respected as the people who don't talk as much. In fact, when those people finally do talk, others listen, because they think they must have something significant to say.

Choose your conversations and words carefully. Don't "run off at the mouth." When you finally do say something, people will look up from their desks, stop doodling, and listen to you. Just make sure that their interest is rewarded.

Don't think you have to fill the air with words. Say what you mean, mean what you say, and then shut up. If you don't know about a subject or have nothing relevant to add to a discussion, don't say something just to be a participant in the conversation. When you open your mouth, everyone will realize that you truly don't know.

On the other hand, if you know that you know, don't be afraid to speak your piece! We have too many people now who are afraid to challenge those talking heads who have no substance.

Than to **Open** **Your Mouth** and Remove **All** **Doubt**

Don't Let Your Mouth
Write a Check Your Behind
Can't Cash

In past generations, it was almost suicidal to even consider speaking back to your parents. Many times I would voice my opinion and my mother would make it clear that I was treading on weak ground. The real question was whether I was willing to accept the punishment or pain that came with what I was saying. Sometimes, our mouths can get us in a world of trouble that is very difficult to escape from after the fact.

In the aftermath of Katrina, I lost a tenured faculty position at Tulane when the President of the University decided to eliminate the engineering program. Since that time, whenever I criticize Tulane publicly for its lack of commitment to the community, people call it "sour grapes." What those people don't understand is that I was criticizing Tulane pre-Katrina and that my mouth may have written such a check. However, when I started speaking out on Tulane's shortcomings my behind was prepared for the consequences, and the (lack of a) check from Tulane didn't hurt me or, more importantly, my family.

I counted the cost of speaking up for what was and is right. I fully and joyfully accept the cost. Tulane didn't know that my mouth was and still is writing the checks to take care of me and mine! When a man buys your tongue, he controls your thoughts and actions. So you better count the cost of opening your mouth.

...count the cost...

Luke 14:28

161

Well Done is Better Than Well Said

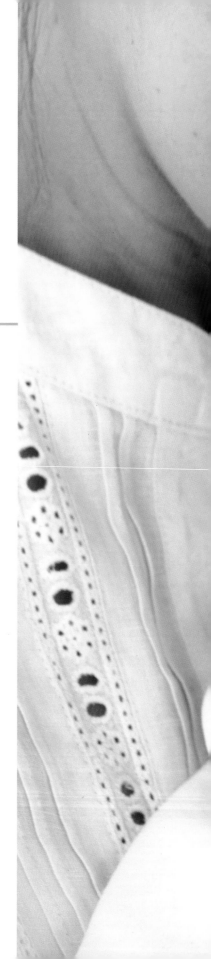

Opinions are like derrières—everyone has one. Everyone knows what you should do. Going out and showing the world via example is the best advice you can give. Stop telling everyone what you are going to do; focus and show the world what you have accomplished. Most speakers today are spouting theory that they have never tried to implement. Show me what you have done before you tell me what to do.

My motto is that I live the life I speak about, and speak about the life that I live. Never try to convince someone to do what you have not done. Many children are confused because they have adults, parents, and others telling them what to do when the older person has not done it or even tried it. Like Gandhi said, "Be the change you want to see in the world." In essence, it is always better to see a good sermon than to hear one. At the end of the day, I reiterate, let your works (not your words) speak for you. Do something!

For a dream cometh through the multitude of business; and a fool's voice is known by multitude of words.

Ecclesiastes 5:3

163

Money

How Do You Acquire, Manage, and View Your Finances?

Though money can't buy the happiness that comes from outstanding moral character, strong relationships, or achieving your dreams, it is an important aspect of life. In a capitalistic system, right after oxygen, you better have some money—and your money must be handled wisely and with great care.

Don't be greedy. I know many people who, because they wanted more and more money, held onto their stock as it continued to rise in value and then cringed when they saw it rapidly fall. Be appreciative of the winnings you get, because greed will never serve you well. Greed is a disease that cannot be cured with more money, and it has killed many successful people spiritually. Many people with money are not happy, because the disease of greed keeps them from enjoying what they have; instead, it keeps them focused on what they don't have.

Don't spend too much money on one thing. I never put all my money into one investment—as my grandma always said, "Never put all your eggs in one basket." I know that I am safe, even if one of my investments fails.

I have heard people say, "money talks." I always ask, "Does it tell the truth?" Many people use money, or the illusion of having money, to mask other personal and moral shortcomings. Don't let your money—or the lack thereof—determine your self worth or image. It is your character, morals, and actions, and not your money, that determines who you are; however, act judiciously with your money, and spend it wisely so that your needs (and your family's needs) can be met. Save and invest in your future!

A Penny Saved is a Penny Earned

We often hear about multimillion dollar entertainers and athletes filing for bankruptcy and wonder—how could that happen? This life is very simple, but it becomes very difficult when we deviate from the simple proverbs or truths quoted in this book. One thing that I was taught is that if you spend more money than you make, then you are broke. The amount does not matter; it is your actions on the back end that ultimately determine your financial acumen. Therefore, we should always save some amount of what we are making and become more concerned about unnecessary, conspicuous spending. Start saving even if it is a penny a day. A penny saved for every minute of every day for one year will yield you $5,256.00. Consider this amount over a lifetime with compound interest and you have to wonder why all of us are not rich from inheritance. Make sure you are saving for your children's children.

Go to the ant, you sluggard; consider its ways and be wise! It has no commander, no overseer or ruler, yet it stores its provisions in summer and gathers its food at harvest.

Proverbs 6:6-8, NIV

Always Keep a Dry Stick of Wood for a Rainy Day

Americans are probably the biggest consumers in the world. At the turn of the 20th century, we were a very frugal nation. Grandmothers were notorious for having died with thousands of dollars buried in the backyard or under the mattress. Especially after the hardship experienced during the Great Depression, Americans became very frugal, but somewhere we lost our way and we have become a spend-and-charge nation. We have gone from the greatest creditor nation in the world to the greatest debtor nation. Individuals are so far in debt that they really do not know how the experience will end. My father always taught me to save for a rainy day. Like the booming internet days of the 90s, things eventually turn. The world economy and your personal economy will not both go in cycles. Even birds that soar high must one day return to the ground. If you save when the days are sunny, you will definitely be prepared for the rainy days.

Don't Spend All Your Money in One Place

When I was a kid, every now and then we'd get the chance to go to the amusement park. "Don't spend all your money in one place," my mother would warn as we'd run away, just excited to be out of the house and in such a fun place. Invariably, I'd find myself lured by all the games—you know, the ones that are all but impossible to win but look so easy? I'd spend my money on those games and find myself broke three-quarters of the way through the day. By then, I'd be hungry and have to ask my friends for money just to buy some food before the park closed for the day—because I didn't dare go back to my mother, who I knew from experience would only say, "Didn't I tell you not to spend your money in one place?"

It was a good lesson. As you go through life, you'll be tempted to spend money in a lot of places, but only one place at a time. You'll want to buy a car. You'll want to buy a house and some furniture. You also may want to pay things like your cell phone bill, and your utilities, and your credit card bills. So when you go to make that first car purchase, don't spend the maximum that the car salesperson says you can spend. They don't know what your budget looks like; only you know that. The same can be said about your home purchase. The common rule is that you can afford 2 or 3 times your income. Don't believe it for a minute. Spending money like that will only mean you'll be living on the floor of that big house, with nothing to sit on and nothing to eat!

Be prudent with your money. Make sure you are looking at the whole picture, not just one thing.

But don't begin until you count the cost. For who would begin construction of a building without first calculating the cost to see if there is enough money to pay the bills?

Luke 14:28 NLT

169

Look here, you who say, "Today or tomorrow we are going to a certain town and will stay there a year. We will do business there and make a profit." How do you know what your life will be like tomorrow? Your life is like the morning fog—it's here a little while, then it's gone. What you ought to say is, "If the LORD wants us to, we will live and do this or that." Otherwise you will be boasting about your own plans, and all such boasting is evil.

James 4:13-16 NLT

Don't Count Your Chickens Before They Hatch

The bull market of the late 1990's had everyone talking. People would buy stock one day and then go look at houses and boats they were going to buy the next day. Everyone was on their way to getting rich overnight. The entire episode reminded me of lemmings following each other off of a cliff. I had been investing in and studying the stock market since 1992, but now everyone was a master, picking stocks and getting rich overnight. For me, I knew the crowd was never right, but eventually I got swept away and placed money in speculative stock I knew had no history or earnings. Eventually, people became very "leveraged," meaning they borrowed money to buy stocks, hoping they would hit a certain target. People bought houses, cars, and yachts on stock "options"—they'd pay dearly for the right to buy shares of stock at one price, again hoping the price would go up and they could sell at a profit later. In either case, the money they spent was money they really didn't have yet. When the bottom fell out of the market, repossessions and foreclosures hit an all-time high across the nation. People were counting money (chickens) before they had it (before they hatched).

The subprime mortgage debacle of more recent times is another good example. For years, home prices did nothing but go up. When that trend sustained for a while, people started buying homes without looking at terms. They did "no money down" deals, they agreed to excessively high interest rates and "balloon" loans just to get into a home that many thought they would be able to sell at a profit not many years hence. They counted their chickens, and the chickens never hatched.

Grandma had it right. She may not have been a millionaire, but she never went hungry, she always had a "little something" tucked away, and she never took unwise risks with her resources.

Money Talks, Bullsh*t Walks

It is said that the Scriptures have more verses on money than they do about any other topic. Your attitude toward the handling of money tells people more about your character than anything else.

It's true. Money does talk. The way you spend it tells people what you value. The way you acquire it tells people about your character. They way you give it tells people about your generosity. The money you put "on the table" in a business venture or investment tells people about your commitment.

Let's take a look at a couple of the ancient biblical characters. We have Abraham, who helped an ancient king win a war but refused to take "booty" from him because he didn't want to be beholden to anyone except God. At the other end of the spectrum we have the widow that Jesus speaks about, who put into the temple treasury all that she had.

What does money say about you?

While Jesus was in the Temple, he watched the rich people putting their gifts into the collection box. Then a poor widow came by and dropped in two pennies. "I assure you," he said, "this poor widow has given more than all the rest of them. For they have given a tiny part of their surplus, but she, poor as she is, has given everything she has."

Luke 21:1-4

173

A Fool & His Gold Will Soon Be Parted

Have you ever wondered about people who win those big, million-dollar plus lotteries? Think their lives are so much better than yours? Ever wish you could win?

Well, consider this: some research suggests that one-third of lottery winners are either in serious financial trouble or bankrupt within five years. And think about all of the sports figures who ran through tens of millions of dollars with nothing to show for it.

And just look at some of our wealthy athletes. Sure, they have money. But do they have the intelligence to manage it so that their money takes care of them forever? Michael Vick had money, but he decided to act foolishly, and the consequences were disastrous. He allowed his home to be used for illegal dog fights, was found out, and served time for something he probably thought he'd never get caught doing.

It really doesn't matter how much you make. It's always been, and always will be, how much you spend of what you make that draws the fine line between wealth and poverty, not to mention how wisely you manage the rest of your life so that you can enjoy what your money affords you.

Your **Heart** is Where Your **Treasure** is

People claim to care about many things. Well, words are cheap. Show me where you put, spend, lose, throw, or invest your money and I would say that is where your heart is. Everyone claims to care about the children. They say that the children of our nation are suffering like they never have in a free country. It seems many working on behalf of the children might need to consider a change in profession, as the results point to some serious issues. Many churches and professional organizations have programs for children, but the budgets for those programs are always secondary to the main meeting, staffing, or adult programs. The children are the afterthought. If the children were our heart, our future, and our focus, that's where our treasure would be.

Likewise, we can check ourselves in the same way. Examine your own spending patterns; what does your allocation of finances say about your priorities? Do you spend your money on clothes and cars or do you invest it in your own betterment—books, education, travel—or the betterment of your family? Going further, are you investing in charitable endeavors that have lasting value: endeavors that improve people's lives in the long term? Check your government, check your employer, and your church. But first, check yourself.

Wherever your treasure is, there the desires of your heart will also be.

Matthew 6:21 NLT

Teach those who are rich in this world not to be proud and not to trust in their money, which is so unreliable. Their trust should be in GOD, who richly gives us all we need for our enjoyment. Tell them to use their money to do good. They should be rich in good works and generous to those in need, always being ready to share with others. By doing this they will be storing up their treasure as a good foundation for the future so that they may experience true life.

1 Timothy 6:17-19 NLT

Pigs Get Fat, Hogs get Slaughtered

I will never forget the 1987 movie *Wall Street* when Michael Douglas was speaking at the corporation's board meeting and proclaimed: "Greed is good." "This country was built on greed," he said. Eventually, it was that greed that destroyed him. Many people are missing their dreams or destroying their dreams because of greed. Greed is a disease that cannot be cured with additional money or stuff—because when is enough enough? So these greedy individuals continue to accumulate to their own detriment. Even the Bible asks, "What does a man gain if he conquers the world but loses his soul?" Many men have become rich never having the opportunity to taste love, family, and happiness—these riches cannot be gained with money. It is okay to be a pig and eat your fair share, but it is greed that gets the fat hog killed first every time.

This phrase is also a prudent investment principle. I know people who watched their stocks go up and up and then held them all the way back down, hoping that they would go up even further later. Instead of being a "pig" and taking the winnings they had, they tried to "hog" the stock by hoping against hope that their dreams would come true.

Greed is NEVER good.

> He that is greedy of gain troubleth his own house; but he that hateth gifts shall live.
>
> Proverbs 15:27 KJV

179

Consequences &Warnings

Many people fail to see the warning signs in their lives, and it can often lead to disaster. We must act wisely and be alert to the realities of life in order to keep ourselves from facing dire consequences. The recent financial crisis caught many people by surprise because they refused to see the warning and heed the consequences of conspicuous spending. Now, the entire nation is suffering the consequences.

We must remember not to overlook signs that seem bad, because they probably are. Obesity and other preventable and degenerative diseases are growing in prevalence, even though the warning signs are all around us. Lung cancer deaths as a result of tobacco usage or heart attacks due to poor diet and/or exercise are ravaging communities as we refuse to

What Must You Watch Out For?

heed the consequences and change our behavior accordingly.

We must remember not to take anything for granted—life is precious and fragile. My mother passed away at the tender age of 51, and it was one of the most difficult parts of my life. I miss her every day, and I wish that I could hear her voice or taste her food again.

The most important thing to remember is to simply lead a good life. We all will have our ups and downs, but if we see the warning signs and make the necessary changes in an effort to avoid the consequences, our road in this life will be easier!

The Blind
Leading the Blind

If, God forbid, you got sick, would you go to your friend to get well? Of course not, they're just as "blind" as you are when it comes to rectifying health challenges (please disregard this example if you're in one of the health professions, but you get the idea).

This is what Grandma was talking about. She would look at a situation where several people of the same age, the same persuasion, and in the same circumstances were involved in some project or activity—be it work or fun—and see that none of them really knew anything about what they were doing. In this saying, Grandma is giving you a veiled warning, and it's this: if you don't know what you're doing in a given area, go find someone who knows what they're doing. Don't find a friend who knows the exact same things that you know and expect to progress by working or associating with them. If you do, you'll both experience the consequences of your ignorance.

If you watch closely, you will see that there are people who will never be caught hanging around with anyone who has more than they do, or knows more than they do. That's unfortunate. In order to grow and develop, you must have in your circle people who can teach you and show you more. I heard about a professional organization that has a "millionaire club," a subset of members who has achieved millionaire status. Each year this millionaire club invites a billionaire to speak to them. I hang out with people who can see what and where I can't, people who have been places that I haven't, people who can teach me more and open my eyes to things to which I am blind. Check the vision of your circle today!

Three People
Can Keep a Secret
If Two Are Dead

Do Your Dirt by Yourself

How many times have you been told "don't tell anyone" and used that as an opportunity to broadcast your "top secret" information? That should give you a clue. If you don't want something broadcast to friends, family, or the public, don't tell ANYONE.

I know it's tempting to share, and sometimes maybe you can. But the absolute only way to keep a secret is to keep it to yourself.

The prisons are full of people who were exposed by people they thought they could trust with their secrets. The world is full of miserable people who are the victims of friends and enemies alike who just "had" to tell someone about their exploits, good or bad. Be very, very careful about what you say, and to whom you say it, about those things that you do not want others to know.

Everything Done in the Dark Will Come to Light

When there are no witnesses to our less-than-stellar actions, we often think that we have succeeded in accomplishing the deed without being detected or noticed. However, life has a way of showing the world what we have done when no one was looking and usually the outcome is not good. Many politicians and leaders have made unscrupulous deals behind closed doors that eventually came back to undermine their character and moral influence.

Former President Bill Clinton never thought his marital infidelity would come to the light of the world. President Nixon thought the Watergate activity would never be discovered. In tragic and violent cases, many people who killed innocent blacks during the Jim Crow era and Jewish people during the Holocaust have been brought to justice. There are people who cheated their way through college and now can't hold onto a job. Many of us have committed crimes, told lies, or participated in immoral acts that have or will eventually come to light. Yes, I am included. There are no shortcuts!

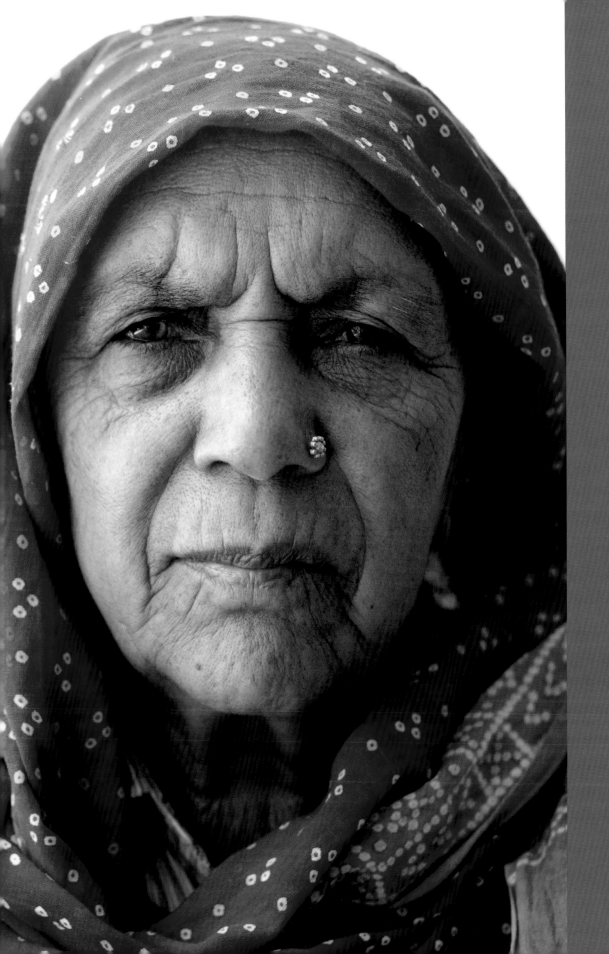

...the LORD...will bring to light the hidden things of darkness.

I Corinthians 4:5

187

Be Careful About What You Ask For—You Just Might Get It

The universe has a way of presenting to us the realities we create in our heads. As a young person I would always hope or wish for something, only to get it and then live to regret it. Don't ask for something unless you are at least somewhat aware about what goes with the gift. Ask to be a leader, and expect painful growth and attacks from all quarters. Ask for joy, and know that you will have to suffer to get there. Ask for money, but be prepared to do the work that the universe puts in front of you. We should think long and hard before making requests from the powers of the universe.

Many people seek out things with no clue about what they are getting into. For example, New Orleans Mayor Ray Nagin, former Louisiana Governor Kathleen Babineaux Blanco, and President George Bush did not know that a hurricane named Katrina would forever tie them together in history. They didn't directly ask for the devastation in the aftermath of Hurricane Katrina, but when they asked us to be our leaders, they asked us for authority to lead during the good and most challenging times. When you ask for something, think about the worst that can happen. Anyone can handle the situation during the good and calm times.

And he gave them their request, but sent leanness into their soul.

Psalm 106:15

189

You Should Not Throw Rocks When You Live in a Glass House

Ain't that the Pot Calling the Kettle Black!

When you point at someone, there are four fingers pointing back at you. Do not be quick to judge others without first examining your house or situation. Many times it is the issues within ourselves that we are so quick to point out in others. All of us have character flaws and should work diligently every day to correct them; however, when we place ourselves above others, we are walking on shaky ground. When we judge others, others will use the same standards to judge us.

It is a principle of life: the thing you focus on reflects who you are. Does any particular shortcoming in someone else—a friend, a boss, a spouse, a parent, or a child—rub you exceedingly the wrong way? Do you find yourself screaming at the top of your lungs about that shortcoming, or talking incessantly about it to others? Watch it; that generally means that somewhere, somehow, you are probably guilty of the same thing, albeit in another form. If your child acts up in school and you go ballistic, think about your own past childhood. If they won't speak up in class and it drives you crazy, it might remind you of your own painful shyness in childhood. The Bible verse to the right explains this idea.

You, therefore, have no excuse, you who pass judgment on someone else, for at whatever point you judge the other, you are condemning yourself, because you who pass judgment do the same things.

Romans 2:1

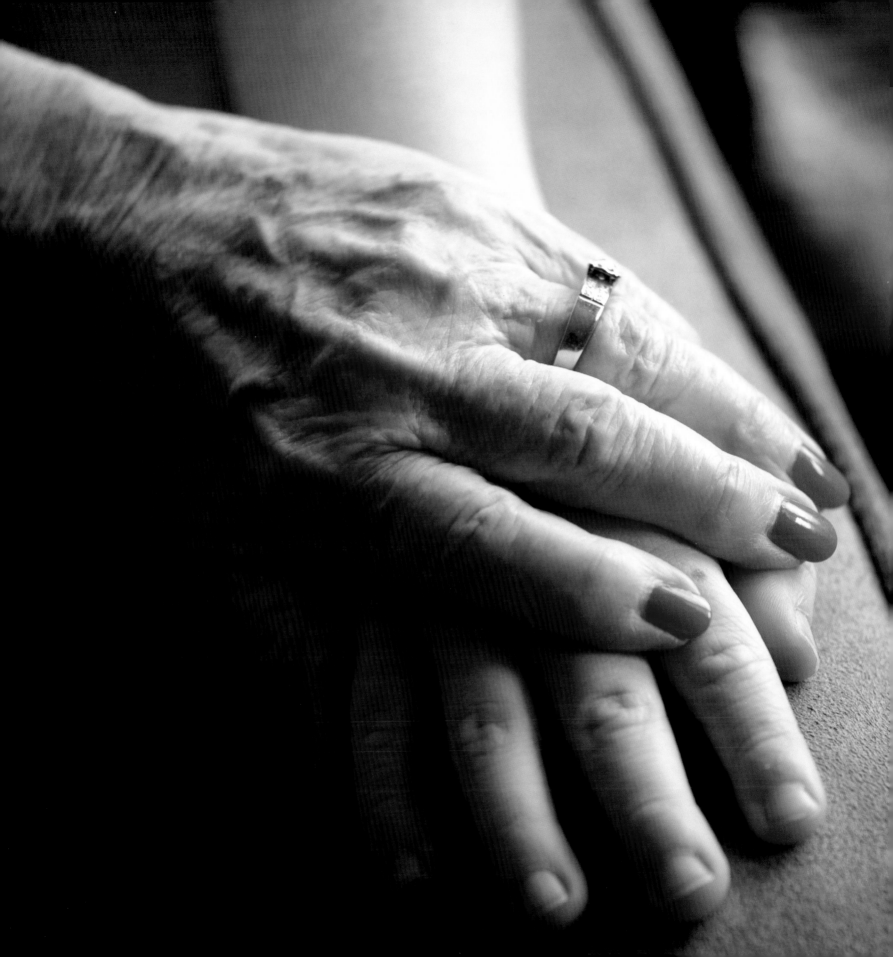

Shadrach, Meshach and Abednego replied to the king, "O Nebuchadnezzar, we do not need to defend ourselves before you in this matter. If we are thrown into the blazing furnace, the GOD we serve is able to save us from it, and he will rescue us from your hand, O king. But even if he does not, we want you to know, O king, that we will not serve your GODs or worship the image of gold you have set up."

Daniel 3:16-18

If You Don't Stand for something You'll Fall for Anything

Character is what you would do when no one is looking. Your character defines who you are and what you are about. It doesn't change with polls or fads, for it is constant, predictable, and unyielding. When your character is weak, you change with the wind. You are one place today and changing your religion the next. You stand for nothing, so anything will suffice for you. A leader, whether in the home or in business, must be clear about where he or she stands, especially on the most controversial issues of the time.

Sometimes you will find you have to take a stand even when it costs you something. Dr. Martin Luther King Jr. once said, "There comes a time when one must take a position that is neither safe, nor politic, nor popular, but he must do it because Conscience tells him it is right."

If You Play With Fire, You Will Get Burned

Many times we find ourselves having to deal with individuals who we heard may have had a shady past. Although we may attempt to judge people on their interactions with us, if we know something from their past we usually allow that to play a role in how we deal with them in the present.

In 2003, ESPN hired the outspoken, controversial, and conservative political commentator Rush Limbaugh. Although many people expressed outrage and concern that Rush would poison the show with his derisive remarks, ESPN promised that Rush was hired to give his opinion from the perspective of a passionate fan and his political views would not enter the dialogue of the show. The commentators were there to talk sports and not pugnacious political views.

Well, Rush did not last long. He resigned after his fourth week under a dark cloud of controversy concerning remarks made about Donovan McNabb, the All-Pro quarterback of the Philadelphia Eagles. As soon as the controversy hit the airwaves, ESPN officials began to close ranks and run for cover. Having hired Rush, their first attempt was to defend his baseless, racist remarks about McNabb's documented talent. Seeing no break in the escalating tide of bad public relations, and amid calls for his head from all corners of the country, Rush Limbaugh saved the ESPN officials from firing him by offering a letter of resignation, which was immediately accepted by ESPN.

I had a slightly different perspective about Rush's and ESPN's debacle. I was neither shocked nor dismayed; after all, his comments were no different than the inflammatory rhetoric that made Rush the king of talk radio in America. The ESPN officials who hired Rush are the individuals who should resign; they knew what they were getting when they hired him. They knew the smoke and fire that Rush generates and they still decided to "play." As a result, they got burned. In life there are just some individuals, organizations, and situations that should be avoided based on their past. You play, talk, and participate with them at your own peril.

Can a man take fire in his bosom, and his clothes not be burned?

Proverbs 6:27

195

...you may be
sure that your
sin will find
you out.

Numbers 32:23 NIV

Where There is Smoke
There is Usually Fire

Growing up, it was amusing to observe my mother catch my sister attempting to smoke secretly. She would go to the bathroom, start the water running like she was bathing or showering, and monopolize the bathroom for about an hour. This would occur on a daily basis, and after she departed, the next person would always report the smell of smoke. She would deny with her life that she was smoking in the bathroom in the face of mounting facts.

This episode taught me that where there is the appearance or presence of smoke, more than likely it came from some fire. Many relationships have wilted under the telling phrase, "nothing happened." One mate was caught in a very compromising or provocative situation, thus giving the other spouse reason to be suspicious. Most of the time it is the smoke from the hidden fire that causes the most problems in life—especially in relationships.

Several years ago people were buying new cars every few years. We watched as people across this country conspicuously consumed and bought houses, cars, and goods way beyond their means. Everyone continued to act as if money grew on trees and somehow magically all of these bills would disappear. The entire nation saw the warning signs and the smoke from this type of behavior. Many of us wondered how people could buy all of this "stuff." Now the fire from which the smoke emanated has ravaged entire communities as the financial crisis has given rise to record foreclosures, unemployment, and government bailouts and intervention. We should always heed the smoke, because we always see it before we see the actual fire.

*If GOD is Willin'
and the Creek
Don't Rise.*

You Don't Miss the Water Until the Well Runs Dry

Students are delightful creatures. I love being a professor and a speaker because I get to interact daily with some of the most interesting people on Earth. However, they are also very demanding and more and more they seem to feel an unearned sense of entitlement. Most professors would bend over backwards to see their students learn, but the students seem very unappreciative of the effort many are putting into their lives. It is a "me first" generation that often misses the precious present lamenting about what they desire in the future, without being willing to put in the work necessary to ensure that desired future. Often, professors tell stories of how students return telling them how now they see the value of their experience they had in college and in his or her class. They talk about how different things are now that they are professionals, with personal and professional responsibilities. When in college, all they had to do was call mother or father and the problems disappeared. Many students do not appreciate college, their professors, or their parents until they leave the safety net and the protection it provides.

On May 31, 1994 my life changed as my mother made her transition. Many of us think Momma will be here forever, that we will always be able to pick up the phone and hear her voice or sit at her table and eat her good cooking. I still yearn for those things daily and wish I could go back and experience them one more time. Sometimes we don't miss or really appreciate people until they are gone.

When the well is empty, we really begin to miss how good and nourishing the water was. We often do not show proper appreciation for individuals, relationships, and institutions until they are no longer available in some meaningful and nurturing capacity in our lives.

If you knew you would pass on tomorrow and you could only speak to one person, who would you call? What would you say? When you come up with a name and what you would say, pick up the phone and make the call. Tomorrow may be too late!

...you will not always have me.

Matthew 26:11

Better Safe Than Sorry

Err on the Side of Caution

> The prudent see danger and take refuge, but the simple keep going and pay the penalty.
>
> Proverbs 22:3

President Bush and his cabinet were convinced Saddam Hussein had "Weapons of Mass Destruction" (WMDs). The CIA and other intelligence agencies had shown that he had possessed them in the past, but no one could say conclusively that he still possessed them. As a matter of fact, many were convinced, and evidence even supported, that Iraq did not have the capability to restore its weapons programs and build WMDs on a large scale. Since the initial Gulf War in 1990, Iraq had barely gotten a plane off the ground; so experts asked, "How could the nation deliver a WMD if it had it?" The President decided in every instance to follow the information that supported the Iraqi WMD claim regardless of how weak or shallow the argument was. He decided not to err on the side of caution, and thousands of Americans now have lost their lives. The military finally ended its search for WMDs in Iraq, finding no evidence that they ever possessed even the capability to produce them since the first Gulf War. Caution was thrown to the wind and the U.S. pretty much lost the world's trust. It will be so very difficult to get it back.

Out of the Frying Pan and into the Fire

One of the marks of human maturity is the ability to recognize danger when it presents itself. But too often we are so anxious to get out of one bad situation that we move too quickly into an alternative, not recognizing that it, too, has drawbacks. Here Grandma tells us to be careful when we change jobs, or cities, or spouses, or friends. Sometimes—no, pretty much all the time—the first thing to change about a situation is yourself.

I am reminded about a funny story a speaker once told of a young man who was tired of his parents nagging him about getting up, making his bed, doing his homework, and generally being responsible. He felt suffocated by their constant demands on him. So what did he do? He decided to join the Army!

Talk about from the frying pan to the fire!

If You Can't Stand the Heat, Get Out of the Kitchen

It takes a certain level of strength and fortitude to grapple with life, especially if you're working in the center of your purpose and trying to make a difference in the world. All great leaders, known and unknown, have this in common: they have to "take the heat." They must wrestle with the finger-pointing and petty jealousies of other people, they have to endure the wrath of the crowd as they swim against the tide, and they have to defend their positions and garner support for their work, their civil or social causes, and their projects.

Any visionary project or initiative is going to meet resistance. If you're not willing to face it, there's really no point in even starting. Our children need to see us take the heat for them when the situation calls for it. Maybe our children are standing on corners taking the bullets that we are supposed to take for them. In the aftermath of Hurricane Katrina, when Mayor Nagin screamed into that radio that the politicians needed to get off of their behinds and do something, he demonstrated the leadership that was needed. It was hot and heated and someone had to stand up because it seemed everyone else was scared to come into the kitchen.

In fact, everyone who wants to live a godly life in Christ Jesus will be persecuted.

II Timothy 3:12

207

Poverty and shame shall be to him that refuseth instruction: but he that regardeth reproof shall be honoured.

Proverbs 13:18 KJV

You Have Made Your Bed, Now Lie in it

A Hard Head Leads to a Soft (Sore) Behind

As an adult, you know not to touch a hot stove, right? You may have had to learn that by personal experience. Now personal experience as a teacher is great, but wouldn't it be better to simply listen to the wisdom of those who had touched the stove before and found themselves burned?

A "hardhead" is someone who doesn't listen to wise counsel. The person who ignores teaching will invariably experience some level of pain. Sadly, it is pain that could have been avoided. The thing is, we should be building on the foundation laid by the generations before us. If we keep repeating their mistakes, we actually keep humanity from moving forward. That's the real tragedy of a "hardhead."

The pop hip-hop superstar Kanye West has a song that says, "Wait 'til I get my money right / la la la la / Then you can't tell me nothing, right?" Well, I think about football star Michael Vick, who had a $100 million contract, or Britney Spears, who is worth reportedly $300 million. It seems they won't listen to anyone, and they have suffered the consequences of their actions: prison, mental hospitals, loss of children, loss of fortune, etc. These are some hard beds they have to lie in, even though their money was or is right! Hardheads trump money every time.

...be sure your
sin will find
you out.

Numbers 32:23

Chickens Coming Home to Roost

Malcolm X made this phrase famous right after President Kennedy's assassination. He pointed out that America's violent and oppressive nature had coiled around on her to bring down one of her most beloved leaders.

It's true: what goes around comes around. It's as true at the individual level as it is at the national level. Be very careful how you treat your family, friends, even your enemies. The only chickens you want coming home are the kind you can eat.

There is an ancient story about chickens coming home. It is the Old Testament story of Joseph, the favored son who was deceitfully sold into slavery by his jealous brothers, and then became a high-ranking Egyptian leader who held their fates in his hands when their land experienced a severe multi-year famine. Here is what they say to each other as they end up in Egypt to beg for food—ironically, from him:

> They said to one another, "Surely we are being punished because of our brother. We saw how distressed he was when he pleaded with us for his life, but we would not listen; that's why this distress has come upon us."
>
> — Genesis 42:21

A few years back—in fact, right after 9/11—the Rev. Jeremiah Wright made a statement for which he was later castigated. He said that America could not expect that its actions to support terror around the globe, heinous nuclear attacks that killed and maimed thousands at Hiroshima and Nagasaki, and mistreatment and murder of ethnic minorities would be without consequence. It was the same thing that some U.S. officials were saying as well. Unfortunately, he bore the brunt of his truth-telling, but that doesn't make it any less true.

Fools Rush in Where Angels Fear to Tread

My family is not the only one with wise women who taught well. I have a friend whose grandmother's favorite saying was, "Believe nothing you hear and half of what you see." It is prudent to verify the truth of something before you rush to respond. We find that especially important today, with the proliferation of disreputable calling operations that phone unsuspecting individuals and offer free trips, contest awards, and low-interest mortgages if they just provide their Social Security number, give their address, or agree to commit to an "affordable" payment plan. The people who rush in fall for the oldest trick in the book: something for nothing. Those who are wise, however, investigate. They ask pointed questions, verify information, and seek counsel of parents, attorneys, or experts before they commit their finances or time.

A simple man believes anything, but a prudent man gives thought to his steps.

Proverbs 14:15

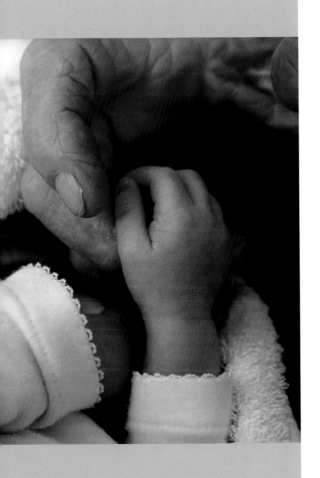

> *But many that are first shall be last; and the last shall be first.*
>
> Matthew 19:30

Every Dog Has His Day

This saying is more than 2,000 years old, so it has survived millennia! It is said to have originated with the death of the Greek playwright Euripides, who was killed when a rival whom he had wronged unleashed a pack of dogs on him. The rival—the "dog"—had his day upon the death of Euripides. Apparently, the rival felt that he was the victim of some kind of unfair treatment by Euripides, and so the idea with this saying is that the person who oppresses others will eventually have his or her comeuppance.

The world is 360 degrees and we have established that what goes around comes around. We treat each other any way without considering that the world turns on one axis and such misdeeds will come back to haunt us. The bully in elementary school is now suffering. The abusive father, the rapist, the robber, the murderer, and the "dog" will have their day to pay for all the pain and loss they have caused. We should not rejoice when people hit hard times or wish misfortune on anyone, but sometimes when it comes, it is well earned. The pain that they are receiving just may reflect the dirt they put in the world.

You Get Out of Life What You Put in it

What Goes Around Comes Around

Life has a funny way of bringing back to you that which you put into it. It is called the Law of Reciprocity. If you give the world love, compassion, support, and generosity, you will usually reap the same from the universe. However, if you give the world pain, envy, and destruction, you'll probably get the same in return.

This is a good place to end. It really sums up everything Grandma teaches us. Your words and actions all have consequences. Your giving comes back to you in manifold ways. Likewise your words do too—we learned about their power earlier. When you understand this, you really understand the secret to life, and that is the principle of sowing and reaping.

So get out and sow something good! And have a good life...

Epilogue

The Values We Hold Dear

All of us can use a guardian angel to watch over us. I think God created grandmothers specifically for that purpose. Knowing that grandma was ever-present in my life made all the difference in the world. "Grummaw," as we affectionately called her, was the glue that held my family together.

"Grummaw" made me feel like I was someone special. She always had a kind word and smile. Even in times of disappointment, my grandmother always knew just what to say or do to make things better. I can remember many occasions where she taught me life lessons through her actions. Her philosophy was "it is nice to be nice." As a result, at points in time, countless people from our community would come to our house for food, advice, or just to keep company. She would always say to my siblings and me that we had to

"love one another the way the Lord loved us." Her attitude of compassion and love made me long to share those fundamental truths with others. I would not be the person I am today had it not been for "Grummaw."

In the African-American community, grandmothers have always been looked upon as the caregiver and transmitter of traditional values in the African-American family. In Africa, grandmothers were considered to be the guardians of the generations. As far back as slavery, it was the grandmother that set the standards for suitable behavior throughout the family. Although the black family as we once knew it has dramatically changed, one thing still remains constant: grandmothers are a source of wisdom, knowledge, and stability in the African-American family. Our grandmothers have helped us

Do not forsake wisdom, and she will protect you;
love her, and she will watch over you.
Wisdom is supreme; therefore get wisdom.
Though it cost all you have, get understanding.

Proverbs 4:6-7

by sharing their past with us and encouraging us in our hope for the future. They personify the values we hold dear—unconditional love, compassion, generosity, and responsibility. Grandmothers are the very foundation of our spirituality, humanity, community, and traditions.

The love and strength that is exhibited by grandmothers is phenomenal. We must always remember those old sayings and words of wisdom. But most importantly, we must remember the commitment to God and family, the struggle and the sacrifice that was made by grandma's hands. I applaud the grandmothers of yesterday, today, and the future. My "Grummaw" made me who I am and left an indelible mark on my life.

Dr. Mackie's book, *Grandma's Hands: Cherished Moments of Faith and*

Wisdom addresses a fundamental need —the virtues of personal responsibility, reliability, choice, trust, and strength of character are so old they have become new again. I hope you have enjoyed every page, every picture, every grandma saying and every little slice of wisdom... if it is important to you what the world looks like in the future, pass these words on to the future generations.

Bishop James N. Brown

Pastor

Second Zion Baptist Church Of Marrero
Marrero, LA

Fischer Community Church
New Orleans (Algiers), LA

Use these pages to record memories of your mother and grandmother so that you and your family can treasure them forever.

Acknowledgments

I wish to acknowledge the generous support and encouragement of:

My wife, Tracy, and sons, Myles and Mason, for the time necessary to think, write, and rewrite.

Joe L. Gordon, or "Uncle Joe," who has never allowed the words and wisdom of his mother, my grandmother, to be forgotten as he continuously reminds us of our heritage. Thank you for being The Rock of the family!

Bishop James Nelson Brown and Pastor Fred Luter Jr. for their contributions to this book and their contributions to the spiritual growth and development of myself and my family. I am a better man, father, husband, brother, and friend because of you.

My family and friends who shared personal pictures of their mothers, sisters, and grandmothers to give this work an authentic and personal touch.

My friends Sheila K. Scott, Diane P. Reeder, and Lynette Doyle for your diligent work and attention finding the relevant biblical scriptures to properly accent the grandma proverbs.

Taz Sugajima and the entire editorial staff at Acanthus Publishing for your effort in creating a beautiful and colorful gift; and a special thank you to Paige Stover-Hague for continuously believing in this project!

My ancestors, who lived, fought, and died so one day we can live! Now your words of wisdom will forever live!

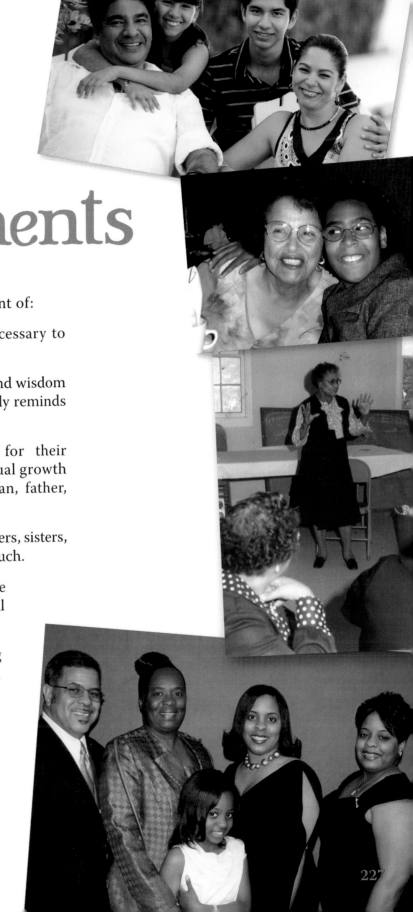

GrandmasProverbs.com

Grandmothers and mothers inspired this book, and we're sure they've been a source of hope and guidance for you, too.

Share your family's wisdom with the world and post stories and lessons from your grandmothers with our online community at

www.GrandmasProverbs.com

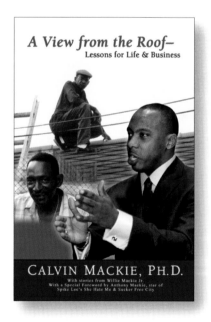

Acanthus Publishing, 195 pages, soft cover
ISBN-13: 978-0-9754810-3-5
PRICE: $17.95

A View from the Roof – Lessons for Life & Business

With stories from Willie Mackie Jr. and a Special Foreword by Anthony Mackie, star of *The Hurt Locker*

In *A View from the Roof - Lessons for Life & Business,* Dr. Mackie brings you right in the front door of his New Orleans home and up on the roof for an intimate look at his hard-nosed but endearing dad Willie Mackie Sr. Through poignant and often hilarious vignettes, each chapter highlights a lesson Calvin and his brothers learned from Willie Sr., and offers step-by-step advice for readers to apply these lessons in their own lives. One part memoir, one part motivation, this book offers an array of practical wisdom that will lead anyone to greatness!

Available at www.CalvinMackie.com